Financial Programming and Policy: The Case of Hungary

Edited by Karen A. Swiderski

IMF Institute
International Monetary Fund
August 1992

©1992 International Monetary Fund

Library of Congress Cataloging-in-Publication Data

Financial programming and policy: the case of Hungary/edited by Karen Swiderski
    p.   cm.
  ISBN 1-55775-304-0
  1. Finance—Hungary. 2. Hungary—Economic policy—1989- 3. Hungary—Economic conditions—1989-
A. Swiderski, Karen, 1955-.
HG186.H8F56 1992   92-20734
                                                          CIP

338.9439—dc20

Price: $17.50

Address orders to:
International Monetary Fund
700 19th Street, N.W., Washington, D.C. 20431, U.S.A.
Telephone: (202) 623-7430
Telefax: (202) 623-7491
Cable: Interfund

Contents

Contents

Preface

Case studies of selected countries have traditionally played an important role in the financial programming courses offered by the IMF Institute. The basic aim of these courses has been to familiarize participants with the issues that arise in formulating a consistent set of macroeconomic policies. Against the background of a rapidly changing situation in Eastern Europe and in the republics of the former Soviet Union, the present case study of Hungary was developed to better address the specific needs of countries in transition from centrally-planned to market economies.

The period covered extends through 1990. Since then, Hungary's political and economic situation has undergone marked changes, an account of which can be found in various issues of the National Bank of Hungary's *Quarterly Review*. The data used in the study have generally been taken from official sources but, in a few instances, the presentation has been modified for expositional purposes. In addition, it has not been possible to include revisions to official data that have been made since the completion of the study.

The various chapters of the study are designed to provide the basic material needed to develop consistent projections of macroeconomic developments in Hungary for 1990, and their implications for the medium-term. The workshop series guides participants in the development of a so-called *reference* scenario, based on an assumption of unchanged policies. The reference scenario serves as a benchmark for developing a normative *program* scenario, which participants are expected to elaborate in the final weeks of the course. Program scenarios are explicitly based on hypothetical policy packages designed to achieve a desired set of objectives. Comparison of the reference and program scenarios should provide an indication of the impact of the policy measures adopted.

Karen Swiderski, Deputy Chief of the English Division, served as coordinator and editor of the volume. Jeffrey Davis, Chief of the English Division, was responsible for overall supervision of the project. In addition to contributing to the text, Janos Somogyi, Deputy Chief of the External Training Division, put the data base together. Other contributors included Angel L. Antonaya, Leyla U. Ecevit, William L. Hemphill, John Karlik and Jukka Paljarvi, all of the English Division.

The authors gratefully acknowledge comments received from colleagues in the European I Department and the IMF Institute. Any opinions expressed are those of the authors and do not reflect the views of the Hungarian authorities, Executive Directors of the IMF, or IMF staff. The authors bear sole responsibility for any errors.

I. Overview of Macroeconomic Developments in Hungary: 1968–89

Background

Hungary is a relatively small country with a population of 10.5 million, and a per capita income of just under US$3,000. 1/ During the 1980s the population declined.

From the late 1940s until 1990 political and economic power was monopolized by the Hungarian Socialist Workers' Party, and the economic system was dominated by the state and socialized cooperative sectors. In 1989 exports and imports were each equivalent to about one-third of GDP; about 45 percent of this trade was with partner countries of the Council for Mutual Economic Assistance (CMEA), largely at administered prices.

Past policies favoring extensive industrialization have transformed Hungary from an agricultural society to one in which industry accounted for about 30 percent of both GDP and employment in 1989. Almost all industry is in the socialist sector. Energy and basic materials account for approximately 25 percent of industrial production. About 15 percent of output and employment stem from agriculture.

The 1970s

An important feature of developments during the 1970s was the steps taken to implement the New Economic Mechanism. Introduced in 1968, it initiated the first comprehensive market-oriented reforms of a centrally planned economy. 2/ While the official plan continued to be important, enterprises were released from mandatory directives and greater scope was given for private and small cooperative activities. At the time of the worldwide economic shocks of the early 1970s, Hungary was pursuing expansionary growth policies. During 1968–73 real growth averaged over 6 percent annually, and convertible currency exports grew by 23 percent per year.

The sharp increase in world prices for oil and other imported raw materials led to a 20 percent deterioration in Hungary's terms of trade over 1974–78. Growth did not immediately suffer as external borrowing financed a rapid expansion in the volume of imports from the West. Between 1973 and 1978 external debt tripled to over 40 percent of GDP. However, following the second oil price shock in 1978–79, policy shifted towards strengthening the external balance at the expense of growth, which decelerated from nearly 8 percent in 1977 to zero in 1980. With demand pressures primarily being reflected in the balance of payments, shortages during this period were prevented and inflation in the consumer market remained limited.

1/ Hungary's per capita income was calculated by dividing gross domestic product (GDP) in local currency by the forint/U.S. dollar exchange rate. Other estimates based on purchasing power parity techniques provide significantly higher estimates.

2/ For a summary of reforms undertaken by Hungary see Boote, Anthony R. and Janos Somogyi "*Economic Reform in Hungary Since 1968*," IMF, Occasional Paper No. 83, July 1991.

The 1980s

From the late 1970s through the 1980s, in an effort to maintain creditworthiness and access to capital markets, while clinging to medium-term growth targets, economic policy was reversed frequently, shifting between expansion and restraint. In the event, output growth averaged a mere 2.1 percent annually over 1980–89, while external debt in relation to GDP steadily rose to reach over 70 percent during the second half of the decade (Table 1).

1. 1982–84: A period of stabilization

With the resumption of growth in 1981–82, the external current account deficit swelled, reserves fell substantially, and creditor confidence waned. Hungary joined the Fund and the World Bank in 1982, seeking their support to help restore its access to international financial markets.

Two annual stand-by arrangements with the Fund were concluded during 1982–84. By 1984 macroeconomic balance was restored, if only temporarily, rescheduling had been avoided, and Hungary had regained its creditworthiness. Notably, the government budget shifted into surplus; balance in the external convertible current account was achieved; gross convertible currency reserves reached the equivalent of 6 months of imports; and growth recovered, although remaining modest. However, the turnaround largely reflected compression of imports and investment; there was no comprehensive effort to address the structural sources of excess demand, low productivity, and the uncompetitiveness of industry in Western markets.

2. 1985–86: Re-emerging difficulties

Macroeconomic imbalances resurfaced in 1985–86 and output growth again stagnated. The deterioration resulted in part from external factors, such as successive droughts and the weakening of important external markets, notably in the Middle East. There were also sizable losses in terms of trade, though these were at least partly caused by failure to change the composition of output in favor of those sectors where foreign demand was stronger. But imbalances were also the result of deliberate policy decisions to relax financial policies. This coincided with a renewed effort at economic reforms aimed at increasing decentralization, enterprise autonomy, and reliance on market-based signals. The greater autonomy provided to enterprises, together with the ready availability of subsidies and bank credit, resulted in wage increases that substantially exceeded productivity growth.

Despite heavier taxation of state enterprises, the proliferation of government subsidies and transfers resulted in a re-emergence of an overall general government deficit in 1985, which widened to 3.1 percent in 1986. These deficits were largely financed by domestic credit from the banking system; 1/ total domestic bank credit grew by nearly 20 percent in 1986.

Reflecting the loosening of policies, the convertible external current account shifted back into deficit, equivalent to 4.1 percent of GDP in 1985 and nearly 6.3 percent of GDP in 1986. Export volumes fell in both years while import volumes increased. With debt in convertible currencies approaching three-quarters of GDP at end-1986, the debt service ratio with the West reached 87 percent of convertible currency exports travel and investment income credits. Despite these adverse developments, convertible currency reserves peaked in 1985–86 at around 8 months of imports as a result of heavy official borrowing in the international capital markets following the restoration of Hungary's creditworthiness in the aftermath of 1982–84. In obtaining new credits, Hungary was also able to improve its future debt service profile by restructuring the terms of its debt.

In contrast to developments with the convertible currency area, the external current account in nonconvertible currencies shifted into surplus in 1985, for the first time in a decade, largely due to a strong export growth.

3. 1987: First steps toward a solution

The disappointing results of 1985–86 continued into the first part of 1987. With the introduction of a two-tier banking system at the beginning of the year, the newly established banks were initially extended generous lines of credit from the National Bank of Hungary. However, faced again with possible external financing difficulties, the authorities tightened financial policies in the course of the year and allowed the forint to depreciate significantly in real effective terms (the cumulative real effective depreciation was over 20 percent in 1986–87). Finally, in September, the Government presented to Parliament a comprehensive three-year program of stabilization and structural change. A major aim of this program was to stop, by 1990, the accumulation of convertible currency debt. As part of the program of structural change, it was announced that a value added tax and personal income tax would be introduced at the beginning of 1988.

There was a considerable narrowing in the current account deficit in convertible currencies in 1987 (from 6.3 percent of GDP to 3.4 percent of GDP). An important reason for this was the improvement in competitiveness brought about by the real effective depreciation of the forint which had occurred in the previous two years. Some of the export gain may also have reflected a speeding-up of export deliveries toward the end of the year following the announcement in November that certain export subsidies would be terminated in 1988. Sizable outflows in short-term capital contributed to the overall balance of payments shifting into deficit, the first since 1982.

1/ Negative external financing of the general government budget deficit during this period reflected repayment of ruble loans used to finance oil imports from the Soviet Union.

After two years of stagnation, growth surged to nearly 4 percent in 1987. This reflected both strong export and investment growth as well as a pick up in consumer demand. Following the announcement that a new tax package would be introduced at the beginning of 1988, there was a run on consumer goods, which was reflected in a depletion of inventories, and upturn in production and imports, as well as in increased pressures on wages and prices.

4. 1988: A year of stringency

The authorities' economic program for 1988 was supported by a stand-by arrangement from the Fund. A substantial share of the initial adjustment was borne by demand restraint. The aim was to reduce the external current account deficit through an improvement in the fiscal balance, tightening of credit policy, a decline in private consumption—for the first time in 30 years—and improved incentives for tradables. Structural reforms included the initiation of a tax reform, a further liberalization of prices, and improvements in the financial system.

The fiscal position improved significantly, adjusting by 3.5 points of GDP to reach a position of balance. Although there were significant overruns in expenditure—largely in subsidies and social programs—these were more than offset by larger-than-budgeted revenues. Credit and monetary conditions were tightened following three years of lax monetary controls. Broad money grew by 2.0 percent, or about a fifth of the previous year's rate, and the domestic credit expansion, at 9 percent, was cut by over one half. Although the overall rate of expansion of domestic credit was deemed satisfactory, more credit was given to households than planned, as overruns in housing credits occurred in anticipation of the introduction in 1989 of a tax on housing finance.

Although in the direction intended, developments in 1988 fell somewhat short of initial targets. The 16 percent increase in consumer prices, which included the effects of cuts in consumer subsidies and the introduction of the value added tax, and stagnant economic activity were broadly in line with program expectations. However, the improvement in net household financial savings and in the external current account deficit in convertible currencies—to 2.9 percent of GDP—were much less than originally envisaged, primarily because of a substantial increase in travel expenditure resulting from relaxation of passport regulations and exchange restrictions.

On the positive side, the trade account in convertible currencies improved sharply. Export volume expanded by nearly 9 percent in response to favorable weather and external market conditions and to the lagged effects of the previous years' real effective depreciations. Also, convertible currency imports declined sharply owing to reductions in consumer and investment spending, and there was some improvement in the terms of trade. A reversal of short-term capital outflows that had occurred in 1987 allowed convertible currency reserves to be maintained at about 5 months of imports.

5. 1989: The adjustment program falters

While output recovered in 1989, the adjustment program faltered as financial policies eased. Developments were dominated by the weakness of the fiscal position and a large unplanned external payments surplus in nonconvertible currencies. Wages also increased much faster than planned—19 percent compared to a planned increase of 6-7 percent—following a liberalization of the wage system in January 1989, which was bolstered by ample availability of bank credit.

Instead of the anticipated small surplus, the overall position of the government deteriorated to a deficit of over 1 percent of GDP. Targeted expenditures were overshot and the collection of tax revenues was markedly lower than planned. In particular, there was a significant shortfall in profit tax receipts, partly because profits were squeezed by larger than planned wage increases, but also because of tax relief and refunds granted to state enterprises and the accumulation of arrears to the government by enterprises in financial distress had been significantly underestimated (see Chapter VI for a more detailed discussion of fiscal developments in 1989).

In meeting the financing requirements of the government, the Treasury encountered serious difficulties. The placement of government bonds and Treasury bills was hampered by an increasing preference of the public for shares and consumer durables, in light of rising inflationary expectations and sluggish interest rates. 1/ As a result, the government resorted to renewed central bank financing on a significant scale, equivalent to about 3 percent of GDP.

The weakness of the fiscal position contributed to high banking system liquidity, which the National Bank of Hungary was unable to offset through downward adjustments in the limits set on credits extended to commercial banks. As a result, total domestic credit of the banking system increased by about 22 percent, or over twice the rate of 1988.

The effectiveness of monetary policy was further undermined by the accumulation of payments arrears among enterprises, due to the belief that they would continue to be rescued ultimately by the budget or by a further easing of credit policy. A rising trend of inter-enterprise credit was in evidence since early 1988, with these arrears estimated to have reached a level equivalent to about 7.5 percent of GDP by 1989. These arrears, which are in effect a substitute for bank credit, further complicated the task of the monetary authorities of managing the liquidity of the economy (see Chapter VII for a more detailed discussion of monetary developments).

Loose financial policies led to a widening of the convertible current account deficit to US$1.4 billion (4.9 percent of GDP), compared to US$800 million in the

---

1/ The increase in shareholding also reflected efforts to circumvent the newly implemented personal income tax. In certain enterprises, workers were provided with shares, whose dividends were taxed at 20 percent, rather than having their full remuneration paid in the form of wages, which were subject to higher progressive rates.

previous year. A small improvement in the trade balance, reflecting improved terms of trade, was more than offset by a further large deterioration in the services account. The latter was primarily due to large travel outflows following the liberalization of regulations on personal imports and travel abroad in 1988. It also reflected larger debt service payments and—increasingly during the course of the year—capital flight, by an underinvoicing of exports and overinvoicing of imports, as well as by physical transport of currency.

As indicated above, problems of excess liquidity were compounded by the shift of the overall balance of payments in nonconvertible currencies from a deficit of US$77 million to a surplus of almost US$500 million. Total trade in goods fell by some 15 percent in real terms, with imports declining by considerably more than exports (see Chapter V for a more detailed discussion of external developments in 1989).

Final Remarks

After more than two decades of implementing reforms, economic performance remained mixed. On the positive side, the authorities implemented price reform early and avoided the major distortions common in other centrally planned economies. Queues and shortages were uncommon. Trade with western economies was significantly liberalized and important institutional reforms were carried out in the areas of banking and taxation.

During most of the 1980s, however, output growth and external reserves remained low while per capita external debt was the highest in Eastern Europe. This, to a significant extent, reflected a failure of the reforms to enforce financial discipline. Bankruptcy proceedings were rarely initiated, the authorities continued to affect enterprises' financial results through ad hoc taxes and subsidies and price and wage regulations, there continued to be a fundamental reluctance to permit competition between domestic enterprises, and the stance of economic policies was reversed frequently. Although the system that evolved was no longer characterized by pervasive administrative controls, the central authorities maintained substantial informal controls. Moreover, measures were often partial, inconsistent, and subsequently reversed.

Table 1. Hungary: Selected Economic Indicators

	1982	1983	1984	1985	1986	1987	1988	1989
	(Growth rates in percent)							
GDP at 1986 prices	2.8	2.1	2.4	−0.5	1.2	3.9	−0.3	3.5
Domestic demand at 1986 prices	−0.1	−0.1	0.2	0.5	2.9	2.9	−1.2	5.4
GDP deflator	4.9	3.5	6.6	6.2	4.1	8.4	15.2	18.7
Consumer prices	6.9	7.3	8.3	7.0	5.3	8.7	15.7	17.0
Broad money	9.9	3.2	5.3	11.2	9.1	10.9	2.0	12.1
Net domestic bank credit 1/	...	4.1	4.9	6.2	12.9	13.0	5.0	14.7
Net credit to general government	...	1.4	−3.6	1.0	19.8	14.3	1.9	13.4
Credit to public enterprises	...	2.7	5.7	9.1	12.1	6.2	−1.8	21.3
Credit to households	...	15.3	16.1	14.2	14.7	15.3	12.0	5.6
Nonruble export volume	6.3	6.4	0.4	−6.6	−3.9	5.0	8.8	2.7
Nonruble import volume	−2.3	6.4	0.4	2.6	0.7	2.5	−6.9	4.9
Nonruble terms of trade	...	1.6	−2.5	−0.7	−7.5	−0.1	1.1	2.4
Ruble export volume	...	...	...	8.3	−0.1	2.5	0.6	−13.5
Ruble import volume	...	...	...	−0.4	3.8	3.7	4.0	−17.1
Real effective exchange rate (REER) (+ appreciation)	3.7	−4.6	1.5	3.3	−10.3	−10.1	2.9	1.0
	(In percent of GDP, unless indicated otherwise)							
General government								
Revenue	59.2	60.9	60.8	60.0	61.5	59.1	63.4	58.9
Expenditure	61.2	61.9	59.4	61.1	64.6	62.7	63.3	60.2
Deficit (−)	−2.1	−1.1	1.4	−1.1	−3.1	−3.5	0.0	−1.3
External financing	0.3	0.5	0.1	−0.1	−0.3	−0.6	−0.6	−0.6
Domestic financing	1.7	0.6	−1.5	1.2	3.9	4.2	0.6	1.9
Convertible current account	−1.3	0.3	0.3	−4.1	−6.3	−3.4	−2.9	−4.9
Convertible external debt (end–period) 2/	44.1	51.1	53.9	67.7	71.2	75.0	70.1	70.3
Convertible reserves (in months of convertible imports)	2.7	4.7	6.0	8.3	7.8	5.2	4.7	3.5
Convertible debt service ratio 3/	47.0	45.4	51.0	79.2	87.1	64.2	54.8	48.2
Nonconvertible current account	−1.0	−1.2	−0.1	1.9	0.6	0.8	0.8	3.0

Source: IMF Institute data base.

1/ Excluding other items (net)

2/ End of period external debt divided by GDP for the year as a whole in local currency units and converted into U.S. dollars at the period average forint/U.S. dollar exchange rate.

3/ As a percent of merchandise exports, travel and investment credits.

II. Interrelations Among Macroeconomic Accounts

Introduction

Macroeconomic statistics are the basic information used to appraise and forecast economic performance. Reliable statistics are thus indispensable to policy makers. Such statistics can be classified into four distinct, but related, categories: the national income and product accounts, the balance of payments, government finance statistics, and the monetary accounts. 1/ For countries in which there is considerable state ownership, it is also useful to have access to the accounts of state enterprises so as to be able to distinguish their activities from those of households. While the various categories of macroeconomic statistics highlight particular aspects of the economy, they should, in principle, use broadly the same basic concepts so as to form an interconnected system that is internally consistent. This workshop focuses on the most important concepts underlying the different sets of accounts and on the interconnections among them. Special reference will be made to the Hungarian data used in the workshop series.

1/ Standards for the preparation of statistics in these areas have been developed by international organizations. The United Nations has published a comprehensive guide for the compilation of the national accounts entitled "A System of National Accounts (SNA)." The International Monetary Fund (IMF) publishes two manuals on the "Balance of Payments" and "Government Finance Statistics." It also has issued a draft "Guide to Money and Banking Statistics" which sets out the practices applied to all member countries in its monthly publication "International Financial Statistics."

Common Features of Macroeconomic Statistics

1. Residents and foreigners

The four sets of macroeconomic accounts relate to an economy defined to comprise all of its residents. *Residents* are those economic units which have a closer tie with the territory of the country than with any other country. Economic units that are not residents are referred to as *nonresidents*. The two expressions, resident and nonresident, need not have anything to do with nationality: a resident of one country may be a national of another.

To define residence, the following conventions have been used. Individuals residing permanently in a country are residents. Migrant workers are residents of the country in which they work if they have resided there for at least one year. A country's government, including the activities it carries out abroad, such as diplomatic representation, is regarded as a resident of the home country. All enterprises operating in the national territory are classified as residents, even if they are partly or wholly foreign owned. Analogously, foreign branches and subsidiaries of resident enterprises are classified as nonresidents.

2. Economic transactions

The macroeconomic accounts represent a summary record of economic transactions. An economic transaction takes place when ownership of a real or financial asset is transferred, or a service is rendered, by one economic unit to another. In most cases, economic transactions involve exchanges: goods and services may be exchanged for financial assets (e.g., sold against money) or financial assets may be exchanged against other financial assets (e.g., a security may be sold for money). In some cases, goods and services or financial assets are transferred without an exchange taking place, for example, when medical supplies are provided free to the population of an area hit by drought. These transactions are also treated as having two sides: the movement of goods, services or financial assets on the one hand and an unrequited transfer on the other. Such transactions may take place either within one country or from one country to another.

In the national income accounts the concept of economic transactions is broadened to include certain transactions within the same economic unit. For example, a farmer may produce food for his own consumption, or an owner who occupies his own house is the recipient of housing services; in neither case is any payment made by the consumer or received by the producer. The recording of such transactions within the same economic unit is necessary, however, if the national income aggregates for production and consumption are to be comprehensive and comparable among countries. Therefore, the farmer is assumed to have sold his production, in his capacity as a producer, to himself, in his capacity as a consumer.

Similarly, the implicit rent of owner-occupied dwellings is included in both production and consumption.

The two sides of each transaction are referred to as *flows*, in the sense that they measure activity per unit of time (this contrasts with the concept of *stock* which measures the amount outstanding of a given aggregate at any point in time). These flows are normally classified as either *nonfinancial* (real) or *financial*. *Nonfinancial* flows refer to transactions that occur in the process of producing or acquiring goods and services, i.e., flows of goods, services, income and unrequited transfers. *Financial flows* include changes in financial assets and liabilities. Many financial transactions have no corresponding nonfinancial transaction, e.g., the exchange of one financial instrument for another.

Real and financial flows taken together record all incomes and expenditures of an economic entity (households, enterprises, or government). For any given entity or sector, the balance on nonfinancial transactions should, apart from statistical errors, be equal to the change in its financial assets and liabilities vis-à-vis the other domestic sectors and the rest of the world, e.g., a family's excess of expenditure over its income must equal its dissaving or borrowing, or if a surplus, must equal its saving or lending.

With respect to the *timing* of transactions, in the national income accounts and balance of payments the convention is to record them when an obligation is incurred (typically when legal ownership of assets changes) rather than when it is settled, or on what is referred to as an *accrual* basis. In the case of Hungary, however, the balance of payments is on a *cash* basis. Government finance statistics, on the other hand, are generally recorded on a cash basis; this is the case in Hungary. Since monetary statistics are derived from balance sheets which are constructed in accordance with the rules of business accounting, they are also, in principle, on an accrual basis. They would, for instance, record liabilities before they are settled. However, since most transactions of banks are carried out immediately in cash this distinction is in general of little practical importance. The main exception in the case of Hungary relates to interest earned on bank deposits, which through late 1991, were paid at year-end rather than when they accrued.

National Income and Product Accounts and the Balance of Payments

1. National income and product accounts

The starting point for the national income and product accounts is the identity between output produced and the disposition of that output. The supply of goods and services in a given year may be viewed as the sum of domestically produced output and imports. The disposition of this supply is composed of aggregate expenditures by domestic residents on consumption and investment, plus the exports purchased by foreigners. In symbols:

$$Y + IM = C + I_g + X \qquad (1)$$

where:

Y = a measure of domestic output
IM = imports
C = consumption expenditure of households, enterprises, and government
I_g = gross investment expenditure of households, enterprises and government (including inventory changes); and
X = exports

Rearranging the above accounting identity, one obtains:

$$Y = C + I_g + (X - IM) \qquad (2)$$

Output, Y, can be defined in several ways. *Gross domestic product* (GDP) is a measure of the total value added in all resident producing units; it is similar (but not completely identical) to the output produced in the territory of a given country. The term *gross* implies that no deduction has been made for the consumption (depreciation) of fixed capital that is used up in current production. Once such a deduction is made, *net domestic product* (NDP) would be derived. 1/

Another output measure is *gross national product* (GNP). It is a measure of the income earned, whether domestically or abroad, by the factors of production owned by residents. More specifically, GNP is defined as GDP plus payments from abroad to residents for services of factors of production owned by residents but located

---

1/ The gross concept of domestic product is most often used because of the inherent problems in recording economically meaningful amounts for depreciation: (1) it is difficult to know how long a capital good will last before becoming economically obsolete; (2) it is unclear whether the correct price to be assigned to the remaining value of a capital good is the price at which it was purchased some years ago or the price required to replace it today; and (3) in some cases the tax laws have explicit rules on the amount of depreciation to be subtracted that have little to do with the economic situation.

In centrally-planned economies the variable used as a measure of output is *Net Material Product* (NMP), which has its origins in the input-output tables underlying the central plan. The difference between NMP and GDP is primarily accounted for by the omission of depreciation and much of the value added of the nonmaterial service sector. Only those services connected with the distribution of physical products, such as shipping and storage and marketing, would, in principle, be included in NMP since such services are considered to be a "continuation" of material product. In addition, nonmaterial services used as inputs in production would implicitly be included as they are not recognized as inputs and thus are not netted out of NMP. Practices as to what constitutes a nonmaterial service, however, differ widely among countries. GDP can thus be constructed by adding to NMP depreciation and the total value added of non-material services, however defined, and subtracting from it non-material services used as an input in production so as to avoid the problem of double counting. In Hungary, in 1989 GDP was 24 percent higher than NMP.

Box 1

outside the reporting country, less payments to foreigners for services of factors of production they own and that are located in the home country. The difference between GDP and GNP is called *net factor income from abroad* and may be positive or negative.

Such payments and receipts relate to investment income, e.g., returns on direct investment and interest earnings (payments) on reserves and financial assets (liabilities); labor income, e.g., from migrant workers in so far as they are considered residents of their home countries rather than the country where they work; and rents on land and building and royalties (for books, films, music, etc.).

As a measure of changes in the income available to a country, GNP is superior to GDP, particularly where international factor income payments are large and fluctuate widely. As with GDP, *net national product* (NNP) can be derived by deducting depreciation.

The definition of output that is selected, thus, influences what is included in "X" and "IM" in equation (2). If Y is GDP, then exports and imports will include goods and nonfactor services. Adding net factor income from abroad, YF, to equation (2) we obtain GNP, i.e.,

$$GNP = Y + YF = C + I_g + (X - IM + YF) \qquad (3)$$

Factor Cost vs. Market
Prices for Measurement of Output

The activity of government in the economy causes a discrepancy between the sum of all factor payments or incomes produced (valued at "factor cost") and aggregate expenditure (valued at "market prices"). Because of the existence of indirect taxes and government subsidies, the final price paid in a transaction is different from the actual receipts of the factors of production involved. Specifically, indirect taxes net of subsidies are compulsory payments to the government which producers treat as an expense of engaging in production. In other words, these costs are deducted in the calculation of the operating surplus of enterprises. They are not, as are direct taxes, paid out of incomes of the factors of production. As a result, in order to move from the concept GDP, measured from the income side at factor cost, to the concept of GDP, measured from the expenditure side at market prices, the amount of net indirect taxes must be added back. In addition, in the case of Hungary there may be significant valuation differences related to, among other things, CMEA trading arrangements and the valuation of inventories.

Output data by sources of income are not readily available for Hungary (Tables 7-8 of the statistical appendix, however, contain output measured at factor cost by branches of economic activity). The figures below are estimated for illustrative purposes using the available information so as to highlight the differences between GDP measured from the income side at factor cost and from the expenditure side at market prices.

(In billions of forint)
1988

1. Compensation of employees 1/	698
2. Operating surplus 2/	383
3. Depreciation of fixed capital	133
4. GDP at factor cost (1+2+3)	1,214
5. Indirect taxes (net of subsidies) and valuation differences 3/	195
6. GDP at market prices (4+5) = (7+8+9)	1,409
7. Consumption	1,004
8. Gross investment	358
9. Foreign balance	47

   1/ Differs from households' disposable income primarily as it excludes social benefits and other government transfers, and is calculated before the deduction of income taxes.
   2/ Obtained as a residual. Part of this surplus is paid by producers in income taxes and what is left over after tax payments represents property income in the form of dividends, interest, or retained earnings.
   3/ Obtained from Table 8 of the Statistical Appendix.

Box 2

There is one other measure of output that may be useful, which is called *gross national disposable income* (GDI). To derive this, the value of net transfer payments from abroad, TR, is added to equation (3) to yield:

$$GDI = Y + YF + TR = C + I_g + (X - IM + YF + TR) \qquad (4)$$

GDI is the total income that is available to residents for spending on consumption and gross capital formation if they are not, on balance, receiving or providing any foreign financing. The importance of adding current transfers to factor incomes to measure adequately income available to an economy can be made clear by considering the residency status of migrant workers. If such workers are treated as residents of the country in which they work, their remittances to their home countries are classified as transfers; if they are treated as residents of their home country, they become factor payments. Using GDI as the measure of income, the income available to the countries making or receiving the transfers is not affected by whether the workers are classified as residents of one country or the other. Net *national disposable income* (NDI) can be derived by deducting depreciation from GDI.

The term in brackets on the right-hand side of equation (4) now includes exports and imports of goods and all services and net foreign transfers. This sum is equal to a broad definition of the *external current account of the balance of payments*, CAB. The three definitions of output and the corresponding concepts of external balance are shown in Box 3.

National Income and Product Accounts and the Current Account in the Balance of Payments

National Account Concept	Current Account Definition
Gross domestic product	Exports and imports of goods and nonfactor services
Gross national product	Exports and imports of goods and services
National disposable income	Exports and imports of goods and services, and unrequited transfers

Box 3

17

Equation (2), (3), and (4) demonstrate that, whatever the definition of output that is used, any external imbalance must be reflected in a domestic imbalance in which residents' expenditure on domestic and foreign goods and services—the sum of consumption and investment expenditure, which is often called *absorption*—either exceeds or falls short of domestic output.

Rearranging equation (4):

$$GDI - A = X - IM + YF + TR \qquad (5)$$
$$= CAB$$

where:

A = residents' expenditure on domestic and foreign goods and services, i.e., $C + I_g$

Alternatively, the domestic imbalance can be rewritten in terms of an imbalance between saving and investment.

Given the definition of GDI, *gross saving*, S_g, can be defined as that part of GDI not consumed:

$$S_g = GDI - C \qquad (6)$$

Substituting equation (6) into (4):

$$S_g - I_g = X - IM + YF + TR \qquad (7)$$
$$= CAB$$

Equation (7) indicates that to the extent that investment exceeds saving, it will be reflected in an external current account deficit. It should be emphasized that equations (5) and (7) are identities. Without additional information, no inference can be made from these equations as to whether the source of the imbalance was external (e.g., terms of trade deterioration) or domestic (e.g., expansionary financial policies).

Table 1 summarizes the various product and income concepts and the uses of disposable income as applied to the Hungarian economy in 1987–88. National product and income concepts were derived by adding to GDP (the measure of output conventionally used in Hungary) net investment income from abroad and external transfers as recorded in the balance of payments. [1] Line 15 indicates that the excess of investment over saving was Ft −24 billion in 1988 and Ft −2.7 billion in 1988. While in principle these figures should be equal to the external current account deficit as recorded in the balance of payments, in practice they were not, particularly in 1988.

---

[1] This may not fully reflect net factor incomes from abroad since data for labor income and income from property other than investment are not separately identified in the balance of payments.

Table 1. Hungary: Relationship of Income and Product Concepts

(In billions of forint at current market prices)

	1987	1988
1. Gross domestic product (GDP)	1,226.4	1,408.8
2. Consumption of fixed capital	127.6	132.6
3. Net domestic product (NDP) (1) − (2)	1,098.8	1,276.2
4. Net factor income from abroad	−48.2	−55.1
5. Net national product (NNP) (3) + (4)	1,050.6	1,221.1
6. Consumption of fixed capital	127.6	132.6
7. Gross national product (GNP) (1) + (4)	1,178.2	1,353.7
8. Net current transfers from abroad	4.9	5.9
9. Net disposable income (NDI) (5) + (8)	1,055.5	1,227.0
10. Consumption (−)	−879.6	−1,004.1
11. Saving, net (9) + (10)	175.9	222.9
12. Consumption of fixed capital	127.6	132.6
13. Saving, gross (11) + (12)	303.5	355.5
14. Gross capital formation (−)	−327.5	−358.2
Fixed capital	(303.5)	(295.6)
Change in inventories	(24.0)	(62.6)
15. Balance on nonfinancial transactions (foreign balance, national accounts basis) (13)+(14)	−24.0	−2.7
Memorandum item:		
16. Current account of the balance of payments	−31.8	−28.8

Source: IMF Institute data base.

What accounts for these discrepancies? The Hungarian balance of payments is recorded on a cash basis, whereas the national accounts are recorded on an accrual basis. This could lead to substantial differences because of leads and lags in payment settlements. For example, if certain goods are exported in December but payment is not received until February of the following year, the national accounts would record the transaction in the year they were shipped while the balance of payments would record it in the following year. There may also be differences in coverage, valuation, and in classification. 1/ Finally, there may be statistical errors. Discrepancies such as those described above make it more difficult to appraise and forecast the economic performance of an economy by reducing the reliability of the statistical information. This is particularly so when there are large year-to-year swings in the size of these discrepancies.

It is useful to rewrite equation (7) in terms of the contributions of the different sectors of the economy to total saving. The conventional approach is to distinguish the government's position from that of the rest of the economy: the intention here is to separate the net saving of the government, which broadly speaking are under the authorities' control, and the net saving of the private sector which the authorities can influence only indirectly through various policy measures. In countries where state ownership of enterprises dominates and where the authorities can resort to extensive administrative controls over these enterprises, a different classification may be more appropriate in which the positions of households and enterprises are separately identified to reflect their different behavior. Sectorizing equation (7):

$$(S_{gH} - I_{gH}) + (S_{gE} - I_{gE}) + (S_{gG} - I_{gG}) = CAB \qquad (8)$$

where:

$$
\begin{aligned}
S_{gH} &= \text{gross saving of households} \\
I_{gH} &= \text{gross investment of households} \\
S_{gE} &= \text{gross saving of enterprises} \\
I_{gE} &= \text{gross investment of enterprises} \\
S_{gG} &= \text{gross saving of government} \\
I_{gG} &= \text{gross investment of government}
\end{aligned}
$$

Procedures for calculating the sectoral nonfinancial transactions balances for the case of Hungary are discussed later in this chapter. It should, nevertheless, be noted here that the nonfinancial transactions balance of the government is equal to the overall budget balance after adjusting for capital transfers and net lending.

1/ Hungarian practice is to classify in the national accounts certain external transactions as domestic transactions. Specifically, private consumption is defined on a territorial basis rather than by residency. For purposes of this workshop series, an attempt was made to adjust the data to conform with the residency concept by subtracting foreign travel expenditures made in Hungary from private consumption and adding Hungarian travel expenditures made abroad to private consumption, with a corresponding adjustment made to the foreign balance. The travel data were obtained from the balance of payment accounts, which uses a cash basis rather than an accrual basis. It is likely that the territory versus residency basis produces other inconsistencies in the reporting of the external balance.

For purposes of economic analysis, equation (7) and (8) are frequently expressed in terms of proportions to total income or output so as to indicate the relative size of the imbalances of each sector as well as to facilitate inter-year comparisons. Moreover, by focusing on these ratios, the policy effort that needs to be implemented toward, for example, raising the rate of investment and an economy's domestic saving effort, can more clearly be measured.

For example, using the figures in Table 1 one can derive the gross saving and investment ratios for Hungary in relation to GDP [lines 13 and 14, respectively, divided by line 1]. Notably, gross saving increased from 24.7 percent of GDP in 1987 to 25.2 percent of GDP in 1988 while gross investment, despite increasing in absolute terms, fell from 26.7 percent of GDP in 1987 to 25.2 percent of GDP in 1988. The result was an improvement in the foreign balance, as measured in the national accounts, of 2 percentage points, i.e., from a deficit 2 percent of GDP to virtual balance.

As noted earlier, the external current account balance, as recorded in the balance of payments, shows somewhat different figures. Notably, the external current account deficit fell from only 2.6 percent of GDP to 2.0 percent of GDP [line 16 divided by line 1]. For reasons already discussed, such divergences could raise questions as to whether, on the one hand, the improvement in saving or decline in investment are overestimated in the national accounts or, on the other, the external accounts of the balance of payments underestimate the economy's improved position vis-à-vis the rest of the world. Answers to these questions carry policy implications.

Tables 7–10 of the Statistical Appendix provide data on the national accounts of Hungary. Tables 7 and 8 classify GDP by branches of economic activity (at factor cost) in constant and in current prices, respectively. Tables 9 and 10 present output from the expenditure side (at market prices) also in both constant and current prices. Chapter IV discusses issues relevant to *forecasting output and prices*.

2. Balance of payments

The *balance of payments* comprises the *external current account balance*, i.e., a record of transactions of residents with foreigners in goods, services and unrequited transfers (as discussed in the previous section), and the *capital account balance*, which provides summary statistics on the change in the net foreign asset position of domestic residents arising from transactions such as external borrowing or repayments, foreign direct investment, and short term capital movements.

The balance of payments recording system takes the form of a double-entry accounting system, in which each transaction is reflected in both a credit and a debit entry. Credit entries are used for (i) real resource flows denoting exports; and (ii) financial flows reflecting either a reduction in the economy's foreign assets or an increase in its foreign liabilities. Obversely, the compiling economy records debit entries for (i) real resource flows denoting imports, and (ii) financial items reflecting either an increase in assets or a decrease in liabilities. For example, an export transaction in which the foreign exchange receipts are deposited abroad would be recorded as:

exports of goods: credit
short-term capital: debit

Following the convention that credits are indicated by a positive sign and debits by a negative sign, and given that each transaction in principle involves a credit and debit entry in the same amount, the sum of all entries should be zero. In practice, however, information on the debit and credit components of a transaction is usually obtained from different statistical sources. Deficiencies in coverage, as well as variation in the time of record and in the methods used for valuing transactions, necessitate the insertion of a balancing item in the accounts. This is usually referred to as *net errors and omissions*.

How then can one talk of an overall balance of payments surplus or deficit when the sum of all entries, including net errors and omissions, by definition equals zero? A surplus or deficit in the balance of payments involves summing up a subgroup of external transactions and distinguishing the transactions within this group (*"above the line"*) from items outside it (*"below the line"*). The decision on where to draw the line reflects a normative view as to what set of transactions best indicates the need for balance of payment adjustment.

The standard practice is to place below the line only the changes in short-term assets and liabilities of the monetary authorities, i.e., *the change in net official international reserves*. 1/ However, if the net foreign position of commercial banks and other economic units is sizable and under the effective control of the authorities, it can be argued that their foreign position should also be placed below the line in the definition of the overall balance. In the case of Hungary only changes in net official international reserves held by the monetary authories are placed below the line.

Insofar as there are limits to the change in reserves that countries are willing or able to accept, an overall imbalance represents an important indicator of the need for balance of payments adjustment. The adequacy of reserves is often discussed in gross terms (i.e., excluding short-term liabilities), and in relation to the level of a country's imports. 2/

The balance of payments identity can be written as:

$$\Delta R = CA + \Delta FI \tag{9}$$

1/ Certain medium- and long-term borrowing of the monetary authorities, notably loans from international organizations that are used for balance of payments support, are classified below the line with other short-term liabilities.

2/ Gross reserves in terms of imports, while a useful indicator of a country's ability to sustain external shocks, needs to be interpreted with caution. In particular, imports represent only a part of external payments. Also the measure does not indicate the size of the potential imbalances between receipts and payments which reserves may need to finance.

where:

$$\Delta R \quad = \quad \text{the change in net official international reserves of the monetary authorities.}$$

$$\Delta FI \quad = \quad \text{the change in net foreign indebtedness of domestic residents other than what is classified as official reserves.}$$

Equation (9) highlights the way in which the balance of payments acts as a constraint to resource use in the economy. Specifically, a current account deficit—which was shown above to be equal to an excess of absorption over income—can be sustained only as long as capital inflows persist and/or net official international reserves are not depleted.

Imbalances in the current account do not necessarily imply a need for policy adjustment. A country might, for example, wish to have a current account deficit financed by long-term capital inflows linked to development expenditure. An important determinant of these flows is the judgement of creditors as to the debt-servicing capacity of the country and how efficiently the borrowed funds will be used. Alternatively, a country might wish to have a current account surplus in order to finance external investment or reduce its external indebtedness.

Tables 11 and 21 of the Statistical Appendix present summary data of the balance of payments for Hungary in convertible and nonconvertible currencies. The current account is divided into balances for the *trade*, *services*, and *unrequited transfers transactions*. From an economic point of view, the distinction between the flow of goods and flow of services is arbitrary: a unit of foreign exchange earned by the export of services goes as far to strengthen the external balance as a unit earned by the export of goods. Use of the trade balance concept lies essentially in the timely availability of merchandise data from customs reports, as well as the quality of trade statistics.

Trade in merchandise is defined on an f.o.b. (free-on-board) basis. This implies that the costs of distributive (transport and related) services performed up to the customs frontier of the exporting country are included in the value of merchandise, while such expenditure incurred beyond that point are treated as shipment *services*. The other major categories of services include travel (goods and services acquired by travellers outside their own country); and investment income (earnings from financial assets, with interest earnings and payments representing a major item under this heading). Unrequited transfers largely consist of government grants of goods, financial resources and technical assistance, but they also include workers' remittance.

The *capital account* distinguishes between short term and medium- and long-term capital. Note that in 1982–89 external borrowing was the main source of capital inflows. The short-term capital account, which includes errors and omissions, fluctuated significantly over the period. Issues relevant to *balance of payments forecasting* are discussed in Chapter V.

Monetary Accounts and the Other Macroeconomic Accounts

The institutions in the monetary system can be divided into two sub-sectors: the *monetary authorities* and the *commercial banks*. The *monetary authorities* usually comprise the central bank, in its capacity of issuer of currency, holder of national external reserves, borrower for balance of payment purposes, mainly from the Fund; and head of the monetary system. 1/ The typical *commercial bank* obtains funds from deposits, that are normally transferrable by check or in other ways in settlement of the obligations of the deposit holder, as well as from central bank and/or external credits. These funds are primarily used for making loans.

Monetary statistics are consolidated at three different levels: the assets and liabilities of the monetary authorities, the assets and liabilities of commercial banks and, finally, the *monetary survey*. The latter is a summary presentation of the consolidated balance sheets of the entire banking system, netting out all inter-bank transactions. 2/

A major purpose of the monetary survey is to allow analysis of the financial aggregates most influenced by the monetary authorities and which play an important role in the determination of output, prices, and the balance of payments. The monetary survey highlights that the liabilities of the banking system to the private sector and state enterprises—i.e., the money supply, consisting of currency in circulation, deposits, and other instruments issued by the banking system—are the counterpart of the sum of net foreign assets (valued in local currency) and net domestic credit extended by the banking system:

$$M = FA + DC \qquad (10)$$

where:

M = liabilities of the banking system (money supply)
FA = net foreign assets of the banking system, including net official international reserves, R
DC = net domestic credit extended by the banking system, including other items (net)

For each foreign asset transaction of the banking system, there should be a counterpart entry in the balance of payments, reflected either in the overall balance or above the line in the capital account. Specifically, the change in net foreign

---

1/ If some of these functions are undertaken by other government agencies, the functions of these agencies should, in principle, be consolidated with the accounts of the central bank.

2/ In countries where financial institutions outside of the commercial banking system, e.g., money market mutual funds, account for a substantial share of financial transactions, a fourth level of consolidation is often constructed to include the activity of these financial institutions. It is referred to as a *financial survey*.

assets of the banking system should be equal to (1) the change in net official international reserves as reflected in the overall balance; and (2) the change in net foreign assets of the banking system not included in the definition of official reserves, as reflected in the capital account.

To reconcile changes in net foreign assets as recorded in the balance of payments and the corresponding stocks of net foreign assets in the monetary survey, changes in the valuation (in local currency) of assets and liabilities denominated in foreign currency as a result of exchange rate movements need to be taken into account. For example, an exchange rate change will change the value of net foreign assets of the monetary survey. Since this change produces no monetary effect, there would be a counterpart entry in other items (net). 1/ The balance of payments accounts, on the other hand, will not have a valuation entry unless they are compiled in local currency, except for changes in the value of reserves caused by changes in exchange rates between the accounting currency and the currencies in which reserves are denominated. In certain countries, such valuation changes would be deducted from reserve changes through a counterpart entry to valuation changes in the reserve accounts of the monetary authorities.

The relationship between the monetary survey and national income and product accounts is not directly governed by accounting identities. Rather, the relationship reflects behavioral links, i.e., the response of components of the national income and product accounts (such as consumption or investment) to changes in components of the monetary survey (such as domestic credit or the money supply). Moreover, changes in output and expenditure will influence the current account of the balance of payments which, in turn, results in a change in net foreign assets, thus having a secondary "feedback" effect in the monetary survey. Integration of the accounting framework with the relevant behavioral relationship will be elaborated in subsequent chapters.

The *monetary survey* and the *accounts of the monetary authorities* for Hungary are shown in Tables 15 and 16, respectively, of the Statistical Appendix. The main headings of the tables are in the format of equation (10). The reconciliation of net foreign asset movements as recorded in the monetary accounts and the balance of payments is made difficult by the fact that the capital account of the balance of payments in Hungary does not separately identify banking system capital flows above the line. It should be noted, however, that gross foreign assets of the National Bank of Hungary were some 10–20 percent higher in 1986–89 than recorded gross international reserves (Tables 16 and 17 of the Statistical Appendix), which mainly reflects the exclusion of certain less liquid foreign assets from the definition of reserves. Movements in these less liquid foreign assets, if excluded from the definition of net official international reserves, should be recorded above the line in the capital account.

1/ Future flows of interest earnings or payments would, however, be affected and thus have a monetary impact. For example, a more depreciated currency would result in higher future debt service payments in local currency terms.

Several comments should be made as regards net domestic credit.

(1) Claims on the general government are shown "net" of government deposits. This treatment facilitates measurement of the impact of general government operations on the liquidity of the economy. Also, the government is the authority responsible for economic policy and, consequently, its decisions concerning expenditure are not usually bound by liquidity considerations like those which apply to other sectors, but on wider considerations. In Hungary, all credits to the general government are extended by the National Bank of Hungary. Net bank credit to the government sector is the most significant component of the domestic resources available for financing the fiscal deficit.

(2) Since the establishment of a two-tier banking system in 1987 virtually no credits have been extended (nor deposits received) to (from) the nongovernment sector by the Central Bank.

(3) Credits extended to commercial banks by the National Bank of Hungary are, by definition, netted out when constructing the monetary survey.

(4) The counterpart entry to valuation changes of net foreign assets are included in other items (net).

Issues relevant to *forecasting the monetary accounts* are discussed in Chapter VII.

Fiscal Accounts and the Other Macroeconomic Accounts

1. The fiscal balance

The operations of the government—through purchases of goods and services, resource transfers, revenue raising measures, and financing decisions—influence the level and growth of economic activity, the allocation of resources between different uses, and the distribution of income. The focus of these workshops is the macroeconomic impact of budgetary operations on income growth, inflation, and the balance of payments. A preliminary indication of the stance of fiscal policy is often obtained from a review of the major budgetary aggregates and the analysis of various concepts of budget balance.

The sum of all kinds of budgetary receipts must by definition equal the sum of all kinds of expenditures. Consequently, as with the balance of payments, the concept of budget balance involves separating out for analytical purposes a subset of total budgetary transactions. Box 4 provides a summary of the main aggregates that enter a budget statement.

Summary of Government Finances

Receipts	Expenditure
A. Current Revenue	D. Current Expenditure
B. Capital Revenue	E. Capital Expenditure
C. Grants	F. Net Lending
G. Financing	
Foreign	
Domestic	

$$A + B + C + G = D + E + F$$

Box 4

An *overall surplus* or *deficit* is normally defined as the difference between total revenue and grants (A+B+C) and total expenditure and net lending (D+E+F). 1/ Inasmuch as taxes and other government revenues absorb purchasing power of the private (nongovernment) sector and government expenditure increases aggregate demand, an overall deficit may be indicative of an expansionary fiscal stance. Similarly, an overall surplus may indicate a contractionary impact. Such an interpretation would, however, need to be qualified by analysis of the type of financing, the structure of receipts and expenditures, and the factors that may be causing the surplus or deficit. Nevertheless, sharp changes in the government's overall balance, particularly when measured in relation to output, may provide an important signal that the impact of government operations on the economy needs to be carefully reviewed.

A further concept that is often used in fiscal analysis is the *current account* surplus or deficit. This is defined as the difference between current revenue and current expenditure, and is a measure of government sector saving. A high level of government saving is sometimes interpreted as representing a contribution to development inasmuch as it allows a substantial amount of capital formation to be financed. 2/

Government transactions as recorded in the different categories of the national accounts can be linked directly to the fiscal accounts. For example, *government consumption* can be derived from the fiscal accounts by totaling current expenditure on goods and services, including wages and salaries. 3/ 4/ This balance may, however, differ from government consumption in the national accounts for several reasons.

(1) In measuring government consumption, the national accounts normally impute a value for contributions to unfunded employee welfare benefits and for consumption of fixed capital. This is a so-called "cost side" approach. The reason for including a value for fixed asset depreciation is to arrive at a measure of the "true" cost of government provided services that approximate the commercial methods applied in the nongovernment sector.

1/ Several other definitions of an overall balance are possible. For example, some analysts prefer to classify grants as a financing item, especially if most other financing is heavily subsidized and not much different from a grant, or if grants finance expenditure that would have been undertaken, irrespective of the financing. Others would include net lending as a financing item, blurring the distinction between financing undertaken for purposes of public policy rather than management of government liquidity.

2/ Government saving calculated on a national income basis may differ somewhat from the amount derived from the fiscal accounts because of the slightly different definitions used for consumption, as will be discussed in the next paragraph.

3/ Government fees and charges and nonindustrial sales should, in principle, be deducted from current expenditure on goods and services (assuming that these fees approximately equal the costs incurred by the government in providing the relevant services) since these would be classified in the national accounts as final or intermediate consumption of other sectors, e.g., fees for museums or recreational facilities as final consumption of households, and payments for government publications as intermediate consumption of business units.

4/ Note that there are substantial differences between government consumption defined in this way and government current expenditure. A principal reason is that the latter includes a large component of subsidies and transfer payments that are not classified as final consumption.

(2) As already noted, the national accounts are on an accrual basis while the fiscal accounts are on a cash basis.

(3)   The definition of government used may differ among the accounts. In the national accounts, the common practice is to use the concept of general government, i.e., the central government, the political subdivisions of a federation, and local governments at all levels. In the Hungarian case, the concept of the general government is used in both sets of accounts.

Government capital formation in the national accounts definition is equal to the acquisition by the government of new and existing fixed capital assets less sales of assets plus purchases of stocks. Apart from differences arising from the second and third points noted above with regard to consumption, the definition of real capital formation in the fiscal accounts would differ from that in the national accounts to the extent of any sale of assets, e.g., through privatization of state enterprises. These would be reflected as capital revenue in the fiscal accounts.

Table 13 of the Statistical Appendix summarizes the general government accounts for Hungary. Government saving declined from 7.8 percent of GDP in 1988 to 5.2 percent of GDP in 1989. Capital expenditure in relation to GDP (including capital transfers) also declined—from 7.7 percent of GDP to 6.5 percent of GDP—which limited the deterioration in the overall deficit to just over 1 percentage point of GDP.

Table 2. Hungary: Government Consumption

(in billions of forint)

	Fiscal Data (1)	National Accounts Data (2)	Ratio (3) = (2)/(1)
1985	193.8	104.6	.54
1986	211.6	116.0	.55
1987	239.7	126.3	.53
1988	302.5	157.4	.52
1989	350.2	186.5	.53

Source: IMF Institute data base.

It should be noted that there is a large discrepancy between government consumption figures in the national accounts and those derived from the fiscal accounts (see Table 2). Although the same concept of general government is in principle used in both accounts, classification differences exist. The most significant one is that the wages and salaries of government employees and other current expenditures incurred to provide social benefits in kind to the population are included in private consumption in the national accounts, whereas, they form part of the government wage bill and expenditures on other goods and services in the fiscal accounts. 1/

The simplest method for circumventing these difficulties when trying to forecast government consumption is to use the information highlighted in Table 2—that the ratio of government consumption calculated in the fiscal accounts to government consumption calculated in the national accounts has been relatively stable. Unless there is reason to believe that this ratio will change significantly in the future, it can be assumed to remain unchanged. Otherwise, the distribution of consumption between the private and government sectors would need to be revised to conform more closely to the fiscal accounts.

Government investment is approximated by general government fixed capital formation in the fiscal accounts since the national accounts classification in Hungary is by decision making authority rather than by the sector responsible for the investment expenditure.

2. Financing

The impact of a given overall surplus or deficit on aggregate demand depends on the way the balance is financed. Financing covers all transactions involving holdings of currency, deposits, government liabilities, and any financial assets held by the government for the purpose of liquidity rather than public policy. Transactions in claims on others undertaken for public policy purposes are normally classified as net lending and are included above the line. An example of such lending is the extension of trade or agriculture credits to state enterprises, often at subsidized rates. Financing of government operations is usually divided into external and domestic borrowing.

External financing is defined on a net basis. For example, it would include disbursements by nonresidents of new loans after deducting amortization payments on outstanding debt. Note that external interest payments are not included as a negative financing item, but are recorded above the line in current expenditure. Each external financing transaction of the government would have a corresponding entry in the capital account of the balance of payments, the classification of which would depend on the maturity and type of instrument used.

1/ This treatment of social benefits in kind in the Hungarian national accounts leads to an overstatement of private consumption expenditure and an understatement of government consumption expenditure. However, it does not create a bias in the derivation of appropriate sectoral saving and nonfinancial transactions balances because the same amount of social benefits in kind is added to both household consumption and disposable income.

Domestic sources of financing are normally divided into two parts: *bank and nonbank borrowing*. *Bank borrowing* can be obtained from the monetary survey, although in practice differences in the coverage and time of recording of transactions may prevent an exact reconciliation of the fiscal and monetary accounts. In particular, it should be noted that the fiscal accounts are maintained on a "checks issued" basis rather than a "cash" basis. As discussed in the previous section, bank borrowing is defined to be equal to the change in banking system credit extended to the government, less any change in government deposits. *Nonbank borrowing* consists of other forms of domestic financing such as the sale of government debt instruments (bonds, treasury bills, etc.) to the nonbank sector of the economy. Information on such borrowing is normally obtained directly from government sources.

In many developing countries, borrowing from the banking system represents a major source of budgetary finance and thus is an important factor influencing monetary developments. In these circumstances, monetary and fiscal policy are closely linked and any attempt to control monetary expansion is unlikely to succeed unless supported by an appropriate fiscal policy. Issues relevant to *forecasting the fiscal accounts* are discussed in Chapter VI.

Financial Transactions: The Flow of Funds

As explained previously, an economy's saving is equal to national disposable income less consumption (equation 6). The gap between saving and investment (including changes in stocks) is referred to as the economy's balance in nonfinancial transactions vis-à-vis the rest of the world, or the external current account balance (equation 7). This balance was seen to be financed by a corresponding capital flow or reserve change in the balance of payments (equation 9).

When the national income accounts are disaggregated by sector, and a record of financial transactions of each sector is added, then each sector's statement is quite similar to a balance of payments statement. Notably, each sector's balance on nonfinancial transactions—which is determined as the difference between sectoral saving and investment—should, in principle, be equal to the change in its financial assets and liabilities vis-à-vis the other domestic sectors and the rest of the world. Since transactions between domestic sectors cancel out, the sum of sectoral balances so defined should likewise, in principle, add to the balance of payments on current account (equation 8). If changes in financial assets and liabilities of a sector are defined in the same manner as capital movements in the balance of payments, then the sum of the financial transactions of all the domestic sectors should again, in principle, add to the international capital movements within each category. The phrase "in principle" is intended to indicate that the identities can be obscured by errors and omissions and other statistical problems discussed earlier.

A schematic *flow of funds* is shown in Table 3. Transactions are identified among four domestic sectors (households, enterprises, government, and a banking sector) and between these domestic sectors and the rest of the world. The government sector is represented by the general government; the banking sector is defined to cover those institutions whose positions are recorded in the monetary survey; and the enterprise sector comprises state enterprises and cooperatives, nonbank financial institutions, and small private enterprises. While it could be argued that private enterprises should be included with the household sector, in practical terms it makes little difference since the size of their operations, as recorded in the official statistics, is very small, and is likely to be substantially underestimated.

Line 1 indicates the sectoral nonfinancial transactions balances that need to be financed. For simplicity, the balance on nonfinancial transactions of the monetary sector is assumed to be zero, i.e., transactions in goods and services by the banking sector are attributed to other sectors. The convention is followed that from the point of view of the sector in question an increase in an asset takes a negative sign and an increase in a liability a positive sign, and vice versa. The sum of all rows and columns should thus equal to zero. For example, an increase in the money stock held by the household sector, which is a liability of the banking sector and an asset of the household sector, would be recorded twice in row 4a, in columns 1 and 4. Thus, the increase in the money stock would appear as a negative entry in column 1 and a positive entry in column 4. Dashes in column 5 indicate that transactions among domestic sectors in the relevant rows do not directly affect the balance of payments.

Table 3. A Schematic Flow of Funds

	Households (1)	Enterprises (2)	General Government (3)	Monetary System (4)	External Sector (5)
1. Sectoral balances	$(S_{gH} - I_{gH})$	$(S_{gE} - I_{gE})$	$(S_{gG} - I_{gG})$	--	-CAB
Financing					
2. External financing					
a. Households	*				*
b. Enterprises		*			*
c. Government			*		*
d. Monetary system				*	*
3. Bank credit					
a. Households	*			*	--
b. Enterprises		*		*	--
c. Government			*	*	--
4. Government domestic nonbank borrowing					
a. Households	*		*		--
b. Enterprises		*	*		--
5. Broad money					
a. Households	*			*	--
b. Enterprises		*		*	--

Table 4. Hungary: Sectoral Nonfinancial Transaction Balances

(In billions of forint at current prices)

	1985	1986	1987	1988	1989
1a. Gross saving	252.6	252.2	303.5	355.5	
b. Households	58.9	69.1	61.3	90.2	
c. Government	69.9	53.4	55.7	109.7	
d. Enterprises	123.8	129.7	186.5	155.6	
2a. Gross investment	258.4	292.7	327.5	358.2	
b. Households	45.5	51.8	51.5	58.5	
c. Government	71.8	70.4	73.2	88.6	
d. Enterprises	141.1	170.5	202.8	211.1	
3a. Nonfinancial sector balances (=4d)	−5.8	−40.5	−24.0	−2.7	
b. Households	13.4	17.3	9.8	31.7	
c. Government	−1.9	−17.0	−17.5	21.1	
d. Enterprises	−17.3	−40.8	−16.3	−55.5	
Memorandum items:					
4a. Foreign balance (national accounts)	34.4	1.3	19.3	46.5	
b. Plus: net factor income from abroad	−43.5	−45.4	−48.2	−55.1	
c. Plus: net transfers from abroad	3.3	3.6	4.9	5.9	
d. External current account	−5.8	−40.5	−24.0	−2.7	
5. Households' disposable income	695.2	747.8	814.6	936.9	1,116.7
6. Exchange rate (forint per U.S. dollar)	50.119	45.832	46.971	50.413	59.066

In constructing a flow of funds tables, each sector's nonfinancial transactions balance must first be calculated. Table 4 shows these sectoral balances for Hungary over the 1985–88 period. Given the lack of data on state enterprise accounts, the sectoral balance for enterprises was treated as a residual.

The nonfinancial sector balance for the economy as a whole (line 3a) was derived by adding net factor income and transfers from abroad (balance of payments data—Tables 11 and 21—converted into forint at the average exchange rate) to the national accounts definition of the foreign balance (lines 4a–d). Total gross investment was obtained from the national accounts (line 2a), with total gross saving being derived as a residual, i.e., (3a + 2a = 1a).

As regards sectoral balances, government saving and investment were obtained from the accounts of the general government (Statistical Appendix Table 13) with the government's overall nonfinancial balance being equal to the overall fiscal balance excluding capital transfers, which were treated as a financing item in the flow of funds (lines 1c, 2c, 3c). 1/ The household sector's gross saving (line 1b) was calculated as the difference between household disposable income (line 5) and consumption, as defined in the national accounts. Data for gross household investment (line 2b), consisting largely of housing investments, is found as a memorandum item in Statistical Appendix Table 10. The sectoral balance of enterprises is then derived as a residual (lines 1d, 2d, 3d). 2/

Table 5 constructs the flow of funds for Hungary for 1988. Row 1 summarizes the nonfinancial transactions balances of each sector derived in Table 4 (shaded box). Government capital transfers, which are assumed to be directed to the enterprise sector, are shown in row 2. By definition, total external financing (including changes in official international reserves) must be equal to the external current account deficit (from both the convertible and nonconvertible currency areas; Tables 11 and 21) expressed in terms of forint (column 5, row 3a: 572 x 50.413/1000). The net external borrowing of the government sector was obtained directly from Statistical Appendix Table 13 on general government operations (row 3b). Net external borrowing of the banking system was derived from the monetary survey (Statistical Appendix Table 15), with the change in the latter position being adjusted for changes in valuation (included in the other items (net) position of the monetary survey) so as to arrive at a better approximation of foreign capital transactions undertaken by the banking system (row 3d). External borrowing of households was assumed to be zero. The net external borrowing of enterprises was then derived as a residual (row 3c).

Data for the change in bank credit and its distribution among sectors were obtained from the monetary survey (rows 4a–d). Domestic nonbank borrowing of the government sector (row 5) was obtained as the difference between the overall

---

1/ While, in principle, capital transfers should be treated as a financing item in the flow of funds, they are sometimes included in the definition of the nonfinancial sectoral balance because of the difficulty of distinguishing capital and current transfers.

2/ While national accounts data do not provide a breakdown of investment by sector, private investment figures were obtained from official sources that are conceptually consistent with national accounts data.

Table 5. Hungary: Flow of Funds, 1988

(In billions of forint)

	Households (1)	Enterprises (2)	Government Sector (3)	Banking Sector (4)	External Sector (5)
1. Sectoral nonfinancial transactions	31.7	–55.5	21.1	–	2.7
2. Government capital transfers		20.5	–20.5		
3a. External financing		–11.5	–8.4	48.7	–28.8
b. Government external borrowing			–8.4		8.4
c. Enterprise external borrowing		–11.5			11.5
d. Banking system external borrowing				48.7	–48.7
e. Direct investment					
4a. Bank credit (flows)	31.7	23.3	7.5	–62.5	
b. To households	31.7			–31.7	
c. To government			7.5	–7.5	
d. To enterprises		23.3		–23.3	
5. Government domestic nonbank borrowing	–0.3		0.3		
6. Broad money (incl. bonds; flows)	–40.0	21.9		18.1	
7. Other items, net (flows)	–23.1	1.3		–4.3	26.1

Source: IMF Institute data base.

domestic financing obtained by the government (as recorded in the table on general government's operations) and net government bank financing (row 4c). The definition of broad money used here corresponds to the concept of liabilities of the banking system to the nongovernment sector as recorded in the monetary survey (row 6). In the absence of the necessary information, it was assumed that all currency in circulation is held by households.

Other items (net) position are derived as a residual. The discrepancy in the banking sector column (row 7, column 4) corresponds to the change in other items (net) of the monetary survey, excluding valuation changes. In the external sector column (row 7, column 5), the discrepancy represents the gap between the external current account balance on a national accounts and balance of payments basis. The fact that the latter two discrepancies cannot be allocated among different financing items has its counterpart in the discrepancies that remain in the accounts of households and enterprises.

As a cross-check, it should be recalled that the figures in column 3 should be consistent with the table on general government operations, row 1 being equal to the "above the line" overall balance (excluding capital transfers) and rows 2–7 to the "below the line" financing of the overall balance (including capital transfers). Column 4 should coincide with the "change" in the monetary survey and column 5 with the consolidated balance of payments expressed in local currency units.

Exercises and Issues for Discussion

1. Exercises

a. Using the Statistical Appendix Tables derive the nonfinancial transaction balances for each sector for 1989 using the format of Table 4.

b. Prepare a flow of funds for 1989 in the format of Table 5. Assume that government net domestic repayments to households is Ft 2.3 billion, with the remaining funds being repaid to enterprises.

2. Issues for discussion

a. Based on the above exercises:

(1) What changes took place in the sectoral nonfinancial transactions balances between 1988 and 1989? How well does this reconcile with developments based on balance of payments data? (expressing variables in relation to GDP may be useful).

(2) How were the sectoral balances financed in 1989 compared with 1988?

b. Suppose the Hungarian government had decided to raise its expenditures above the level actually recorded in 1989.

Indicate how:

(1) the nonfinancial transaction balances might have changed

(2) the flow of funds might have been affected

In discussing these points, alternative methods of financing the increase in expenditure should be considered (e.g., tax increases vs. an increase in central bank credits).

Table 6. Hungary: Selected Economic Indicators

	1982	1983	1984	1985	1986	1987	1988	1989	1990 Reference Program
(Growth rates in percent)									
GDP at 1986 prices	2.8	2.1	2.4	-0.5	1.2	3.9	-0.3	3.5	
Domestic demand at 1986 prices	-0.1	-0.1	0.2	0.5	2.9	2.9	-1.2	5.4	
GDP deflator	4.9	3.5	6.6	6.2	4.1	8.4	15.2	18.7	
Consumer prices	6.9	7.3	8.3	7.0	5.3	8.7	15.7	17.0	
Broad money	9.9	3.2	5.3	11.2	9.1	10.9	2.0	12.1	
Net domestic bank credit 1/	...	4.1	4.9	6.2	12.9	13.0	5.0	14.7	
Net credit to general government	...	1.4	-3.6	1.0	19.8	14.3	1.9	13.4	
Credit to public enterprises	...	2.7	5.7	9.1	12.1	6.2	-1.8	21.3	
Credit to households	...	15.3	16.1	14.2	14.7	15.3	12.0	5.6	
Nonruble export volume	6.3	6.4	0.4	-6.6	-3.9	5.0	8.8	2.7	
Nonruble import volume	-2.3	6.4	0.4	2.6	0.7	2.5	-6.9	4.9	
Nonruble terms of trade	...	1.6	-2.5	-0.7	-7.5	-0.1	1.1	2.4	
Ruble export volume	...	...	...	8.3	-0.1	2.5	0.6	-13.5	
Ruble import volume	...	...	...	-0.4	3.8	3.7	4.0	-17.1	
Real effective exchange rate (REER) (+ appreciation)	3.7	-4.6	1.5	3.3	-10.3	-10.1	2.9	1.0	
(In percent of GDP, unless indicated otherwise)									
General government									
Revenue	59.2	60.9	60.8	60.0	61.5	59.1	63.4	58.9	
Expenditure	61.2	61.9	59.4	61.1	64.6	62.7	63.3	60.2	
Deficit(-)	-2.1	-1.1	1.4	-1.1	-3.1	-3.5	0.0	-1.3	
External financing	0.3	0.5	0.1	-0.1	-0.3	-0.6	-0.6	-0.6	
Domestic financing	1.7	0.6	-1.5	1.2	3.9	4.2	0.6	1.9	
Convertible current account	-1.3	0.3	0.3	-4.1	-6.3	-3.4	-2.9	-4.9	
Convertible external debt (end-period) 2/	44.1	51.1	53.9	67.7	71.2	75.0	70.1	70.3	
Convertible reserves (in months of convertible imports)	2.7	4.7	6.0	8.3	7.8	5.2	4.7	3.5	
Convertible debt service ratio 3/	47.0	45.4	51.0	79.2	87.1	64.2	54.8	48.2	
Nonconvertible current account	-1.0	-1.2	-0.1	1.9	0.6	0.8	0.8	3.0	

Source: IMF Institute data base.

1/ Excluding other items (net).
2/ End of period external debt divided by GDP for the year as a whole in local currency units and converted into U.S. dollars at the period average forint/U.S. dollar exchange rate.
3/ As a percent of merchandise exports, travel and investment credits.

Table 7. Hungary: Gross Domestic Product by Sector

(In billions of forint, at approximately 1986 prices) 1/

	1982	1983	1984	1985	1986	1987	1988	1989	1990 Reference Progra
Industry	344.0	350.3	359.2	351.7	350.0	361.8	362.0	355.4	
Agriculture and forestry	172.2	172.3	180.2	173.0	178.9	174.7	188.6	181.8	
Construction	84.6	86.9	82.4	78.0	77.7	82.3	78.3	79.7	
Transport and communications	80.8	81.0	83.4	82.6	85.5	89.8	91.6	96.1	
Trade	100.3	102.6	102.3	105.9	107.4	114.4	101.0	102.0	
Other material branches	20.6	22.4	23.8	25.5	25.9	28.6	27.6	36.8	
Non-material branches	136.7	139.2	145.7	151.7	155.7	168.1	171.2	212.1	
GDP at factor cost	939.1	954.7	976.9	968.4	981.1	1019.7	1020.3	1064.0	
Plus: indirect taxes less subsidies and valuation changes 2/	79.4	85.2	87.8	91.5	91.5	95.1	91.2	86.9	
GDP at market prices	1018.5	1039.9	1064.7	1059.9	1072.6	1114.8	1111.5	1150.9	
Memorandum item: GDP deflator	83.2	86.2	91.9	97.5	101.5	110.0	126.7	150.4	

Source: IMF Institute data base.

1/ The value of the deflator for GDP at market prices in 1986 is 101.5 (see Memorandum item).

2/ Turnover taxes, customs taxes, and other business taxes, less government transfers to enterprises. Also includes valuation changes and a statistical discrepancy.

Table 8. Hungary: Gross Domestic Product by Sector

(In billions of forint, at current prices)

	1982	1983	1984	1985	1986	1987	1988	1989	1990 Reference Program
Industry	290.0	303.8	329.7	351.9	361.0	399.9	430.3	515.3	
Agriculture and forestry	148.5	153.0	166.1	159.4	174.5	189.3	209.3	235.5	
Construction	60.1	65.4	71.1	74.0	79.0	91.6	96.8	114.7	
Transport and communications	70.5	71.4	74.2	77.7	86.3	94.4	101.2	124.2	
Trade	69.9	76.8	86.8	96.7	108.0	128.1	125.9	157.9	
Other material branches	16.2	18.9	21.9	31.3	34.2	30.4	30.6	37.3	
Non-material branches	103.3	112.9	125.4	140.4	154.3	176.7	220.0	308.9	
GDP at factor cost	758.5	802.2	875.2	931.4	997.2	1110.4	1214.1	1493.8	
Plus: indirect taxes less subsidies 1/	89.4	94.2	103.3	102.3	91.6	116.0	194.7	236.6	
GDP at market prices	847.9	896.4	978.5	1033.7	1088.8	1226.4	1408.8	1730.4	
Less: Depreciation	97.3	99.5	105.7	114.3	121.3	127.6	132.6	151.7	
Net domestic product	750.6	796.9	872.8	919.4	967.5	1098.8	1276.2	1578.7	
Memorandum items:									
Net nonmaterial services	54.2	58.8	68.7	77.1	85.6	105.6	131.5	185.3	
Net material product	696.4	738.1	804.1	842.3	881.9	993.2	1144.7	1393.4	

Source: IMF Institute data base.

1/ Turnover taxes, customs taxes, and other business taxes, less government transfers to enterprises. Also includes valuation changes and a statistical discrepancy.

Table 9. Hungary: Components of Aggregate Demand

(In billions of forint at 1986 prices)

	1982	1983	1984	1985	1986	1987	1988	1989	1990 Reference Program
Household consumption 1/	651.4	653.6	660.6	670.6	681.1	700.3	687.2	744.5	
Public consumption	105.5	105.7	107.1	111.4	116.5	117.1	123.5	127.9	
Total consumption	756.9	759.3	767.6	781.9	797.6	817.4	810.7	872.4	
Gross fixed investment	281.5	272.0	261.9	253.8	261.2	284.9	261.2	274.7	
Stockbuilding	-3.1	2.8	6.3	5.3	12.5	-0.5	17.0	0.6	
Gross investment	278.5	274.8	268.1	259.2	273.7	284.4	278.2	275.3	
Domestic demand	1035.4	1034.1	1035.8	1041.1	1071.3	1101.8	1088.9	1147.7	
Exports of goods and nonfactor services 2/	385.7	412.7	441.4	464.7	459.2	486.4	518.5	530.3	
Imports of goods and nonfactor services 2/	402.6	407.0	412.5	445.9	457.9	473.4	495.9	527.1	
GDP at market prices	1018.5	1039.9	1064.7	1059.9	1072.6	1114.8	1111.5	1150.9	
Memorandum item: Distribution of gross fixed investment				253.8	261.2	284.9	261.2	274.7	
Household investment	...	...	...	49.2	51.8	47.4	44.7	46.9	
State investment	...	...	...	78.5	70.4	68.7	78.3	79.8	
Enterprise investment	...	...	...	126.1	139.0	168.8	138.2	148.0	

Source: IMF Institute data base.

1/ Standard definition: consumption of residents at home and abroad.
2/ Standard definition: including foreign tourism.

Table 10. Hungary: Components of Aggregate Demand

(In billions of forint at current prices)

	1982	1983	1984	1985	1986	1987	1988	1989	1990 Reference Program
Household consumption 1/	505.5	540.0	587.6	636.3	678.7	753.3	846.7	1059.8	
Public consumption	84.2	90.9	95.3	104.6	116.0	126.3	157.4	177.7	
Total consumption	589.7	630.9	682.9	740.9	794.7	879.6	1004.1	1237.5	
Gross fixed investment	213.9	220.0	225.4	232.1	261.2	303.5	295.6	348.3	
Stockbuilding	27.9	17.1	26.4	26.3	31.6	24.0	62.6	96.6	
Gross investment	241.8	237.1	251.8	258.4	292.7	327.5	358.2	444.9	
Domestic demand	831.5	868.0	934.7	999.3	1087.4	1207.1	1362.3	1682.4	
Exports of goods and nonfactor services 2/	336.5	378.4	422.9	459.2	459.2	502.3	574.0	678.9	
Imports of goods and nonfactor services 2/	320.2	349.9	379.1	424.8	457.9	483.0	527.5	630.9	
GDP at market prices	847.9	896.4	978.5	1033.7	1088.8	1226.4	1408.8	1730.4	
Memorandum item: Distribution of gross fixed investment				232.1	261.2	303.5	295.6	348.3	
Household investment	...	...	...	45.5	51.8	51.5	58.5	73.4	
State investment	...	...	...	71.8	70.4	73.2	88.6	101.2	
Enterprise investment	...	...	...	114.8	139.0	178.8	148.5	173.7	

Source: IMF Institute data base.

1/ Standard definition: consumption of residents at home and abroad.

2/ Standard definition: including foreign tourism.

Table 11. Hungary: Balance of Payments in Convertible Currencies

(In millions of U.S. dollars)

	1982	1983	1984	1985	1986	1987	1988	1989	1990 Reference	1990 Program
Trade balance	668.0	773.0	891.0	128.0	-482.0	37.0	489.0	536.0		
Exports	4831.0	4832.0	4916.0	4188.0	4186.0	5051.0	5505.0	6446.0		
Imports	-4163.0	-4059.0	-4025.0	-4060.0	-4668.0	-5014.0	-5016.0	-5910.0		
Services (net)	-1028.0	-755.0	-889.0	-1035.0	-1087.0	-1018.0	-1408.0	-2100.0		
Freight and insurance, net	-222.0	-164.0	-154.0	-156.0	-237.0	-309.0	-299.0	-310.0		
Travel (net)	180.0	167.0	165.0	147.0	199.0	367.0	41.0	-349.0		
Credits	264.0	256.0	268.0	281.0	364.0	553.0	670.0	738.0		
Debits	-84.0	-89.0	-103.0	-134.0	-165.0	-186.0	-629.0	-1087.0		
Investment income (net)	-1118.0	-758.0	-816.0	-833.0	-963.0	-988.0	-1076.0	-1386.0		
Credits	79.0	97.0	128.0	186.0	252.0	235.0	230.0	219.0		
Debits	-1197.0	-855.0	-944.0	-1019.0	-1215.0	-1223.0	-1306.0	-1605.0		
Other current payments (net)	132.0	0.0	-84.0	-193.0	-86.0	-88.0	-74.0	-55.0		
Unrequited transfers (net)	61.0	53.0	63.0	61.0	74.0	102.0	115.0	126.0		
Current account	-299.0		65.0	-846.0	-1495.0	-879.0	-804.0	-1438.0		
Medium- and long-term capital	-43.4	-158.4	1298.5	1692.7	1107.1	1109.8	690.5	1563.1		
Assets (net)	-510.0	-185.0	-43.0	-240.0	-79.0	-84.0	-26.0	32.0		
Liabilities (net)	466.6	26.6	1341.5	1932.7	1186.1	1193.8	716.5	1351.1		
Disbursements	1701.6	1522.6	3102.5	4513.0	4105.0	3364.0	2565.5	3091.2		
Amortizations	-1235.0	-1496.0	-1761.0	-2580.3	-2918.9	-2170.2	-1849.0	-1740.1		
Direct capital investment								180.0		
Short-term capital	-708.0	438.0	-1247.2	-170.0	79.3	-770.8	65.0	-218.0		
(including errors and omissions)										
Total Capital account	-751.4	208.6	51.3	1522.7	1186.4	339.0	755.5	1345.1		
Overall balance	-1050.4	279.6	13.7	676.7	-308.6	-540.0	-48.5	-92.9		
Financing	1050.4	-279.6	-13.7	-676.7	308.6	540.0	48.5	92.9		
Change in reserves (inc=-)	813.0	-635.0	-449.2	-766.4	-260.5	893.8	182.0	251.0		
Use of Fund credit	237.4	355.4	435.5	-89.7	-48.1	-353.8	-133.5	-158.1		
Purchases	237.4	355.4	435.5	0.0	0.0	0.0	221.5	65.8		
Repurchases	0.0	0.0	0.0	-89.7	-48.1	-353.8	-355.0	-223.9		

Source: IMF Institute data base.

Table 12. Hungary: Nonruble Trade, Customs Basis

(In millions of US$ and percentage change)

	1982	1983	1984	1985	1986	1987	1988	1989	1990 Reference	1990 Program
Exports, fob	4974.3	4989.2	4899.4	4483.3	4485.7	5005.7	5833.0	6030.0		
(percent change)		0.3	-1.8	-8.5	0.1	11.6	16.5	3.4		
Exports fob, 1986 prices	4487.1	4774.3	4998.3	4667.1	4485.7	4709.0	5123.5	5259.8		
(percent change)		6.4	0.4	-6.6	-3.9	5.0	8.8	2.7		
Export prices, 1986=100	110.9	104.5	98.0	96.1	100.0	106.3	113.8	114.6		
(percent change)		-5.7	-6.2	-2.0	4.1	6.3	7.1	0.7		
Adjustments from customs										
to BOP basis 1/	-143.3	-157.2	16.6	-295.3	-299.7	45.3	-328.0	416.0	416.0	416.0
Convertible currency										
exports, B.O.P.basis	4831.0	4832.0	4916.0	4188.0	4186.0	5051.0	5505.0	6446.0		
Imports, cif	4512.0	4453.4	4297.5	4353.7	4937.7	5386.7	5313.0	5476.0		
(percent change)		-1.3	-3.5	1.3	13.4	9.1	-1.4	3.1		
Imports, cif, 1986 prices	4474.8	4761.2	4776.1	4902.3	4937.7	5062.7	4715.2	4943.9		
(percent change)		6.4	0.4	2.6	0.7	2.5	-6.9	4.9		
Import prices, 1986=100	100.8	93.5	90.0	88.8	100.0	106.4	112.7	110.8		
(percent change)		-7.2	-3.8	-1.3	12.6	6.4	5.9	-1.7		
Adjustments from customs										
to BOP basis 1/	-349.0	-394.4	-272.5	-293.7	-269.7	-372.7	-297.0	434.0	434.0	434.0
Convertible currency										
imports, B.O.P.basis	4163.0	4059.0	4025.0	4060.0	4668.0	5014.0	5016.0	5910.0		
Terms of trade (US$)	109.9	111.7	108.9	108.2	100.0	99.9	101.0	103.5		
(percent change)		1.6	-2.5	-0.7	-7.5	-0.1	1.1	2.4		

Source: IMF Institute data base.

1/ Adjustments account for freight and insurance, leads and lags, and trade under clearing arrangements in currencies other than the ruble.

Table 13. Hungary: Operations of the General Government

(In billions of forint)

	1982	1983	1984	1985	1986	1987	1988	1989	1990 Reference	Program
Revenue	501.6	545.6	594.8	620.1	669.4	724.8	892.9	1,019.0		
Tax Revenue 1/	420.6	474.3	514.6	515.9	568.7	642.9	760.9	836.0		
Nontax revenue 2/	81.0	71.3	80.2	104.2	100.7	81.9	132.0	183.0		
Total expenditure 3/	519.2	555.1	581.2	631.9	703.5	768.4	892.3	1,041.5		
Current expenditure	440.2	479.9	503.8	550.2	616.0	669.1	783.2	929.3		
Wages and salaries	63.2	65.5	70.4	81.1	87.8	92.9	122.9	141.6		
Other goods and services	99.1	94.6	103.2	112.7	123.8	146.8	179.6	208.6		
Interest payments	9.4	2.1	5.5	3.7	14.1	31.6	22.5	41.3		
Subsidies and transfers	268.5	317.7	324.7	352.7	390.3	397.8	458.2	537.8		
Capital expenditure 3/	79.0	75.2	77.4	81.7	87.5	99.2	109.1	112.2		
Fixed capital formation	50.9	68.9	71.0	71.8	70.4	73.2	88.6	101.2		
Capital transfers 3/	28.1	6.3	6.4	9.9	17.1	26.0	20.5	11.0		
Overall balance	-17.6	-9.5	13.6	-11.8	-34.1	-43.5	0.6	-22.6		
Financing	17.6	9.5	-13.6	11.8	34.1	43.5	-0.6	22.6		
External financing	2.9	4.1	1.3	-1.1	-2.8	-7.7	-8.4	-10.3		
Domestic financing	14.7	5.4	-14.9	12.9	36.9	51.2	7.8	32.9		
Bank borrowing, net	...	4.2	-10.8	2.9	58.4	50.3	7.5	55.0		
Nonbank borrowing	...	1.2	-4.1	10.0	-21.5	0.9	0.3	-22.1		

Source: IMF Institute database.

1/ Including profit transfers from government-owned financial and nonfinancial enterprises.
2/ Including capital revenue.
3/ Including a small amount of lending less repayments.

Table 14. Hungary: General Government Tax Revenue

(In billions of forint)

	1982	1983	1984	1985	1986	1987	1988	1989	1990	
									Reference	Program
Income taxes	106.5	125.4	132.4	108.8	129.6	155.4	184.9	214.4		
Individuals	4.3	8.0	8.7	9.6	8.4	9.5	66.3	94.2		
Enterprises	102.2	117.4	123.7	99.2	121.2	145.9	118.6	120.2		
Payroll taxes	75.7	81.6	114.4	162.2	180.9	190.4	203.2	243.9		
Social security contributions	74.5	81.6	114.4	134.3	141.3	147.8	188.9	243.9		
Taxes on wages and earnings	1.2	0.0	0.0	27.9	39.6	42.6	14.3	0.0		
Property taxes	22.5	30.6	38.8	28.3	23.2	25.2	7.0	6.2		
Net wealth, corporate	13.5	13.0	13.5	19.4	17.5	19.8	--	--		
Confiscation and other	0.4	8.8	17.4	0.2	0.3	--	0.8	--		
Local property taxes	8.6	8.8	7.9	8.7	5.4	5.4	6.2	6.2		
Taxes on goods and services	208.8	223.1	209.1	204.8	220.0	241.9	361.4	369.3		
Consumer turnover taxes and excises	72.5	83.6	88.0	94.0	105.5	127.5	211.8	230.7		
Producers' differential turnover taxes	94.1	94.9	72.7	73.1	57.3	60.6	93.9	65.9		
Import duties	23.1	24.8	24.5	27.6	32.7	34.7	36.3	48.9		
Other taxes on goods and services	19.1	19.8	23.9	10.1	24.5	19.1	19.4	23.8		
Other taxes	7.1	13.6	19.9	11.8	15.0	30.1	4.4	2.2		
Total tax revenue	420.6	474.3	514.6	515.9	568.7	643.0	760.9	836.0		

Source: IMF Institute data base.

Table 15. Hungary: Monetary Survey

(In billions of forint, end of period)

	1982	1983	1984	1985	1986	1987	1988	1989	1990 Reference Program
Net foreign assets	-336.9	-386.4	-427.8	-451.9	-574.5	-728.3	-830.2	-1074.1	
Net domestic credit	742.8	808.5	887.1	963.4	1134.1	1363.7	1483.7	1806.5	
General government (net)	298.1	302.3	291.5	294.4	352.8	403.1	410.6	465.6	
State enterprises	276.8	284.2	300.3	327.5	367.1	389.9	382.8	464.4	
Private entrepreneurs	2.5	3.1	4.0	4.6	5.1	6.9	8.6	18.5	
Financial institutions 1/	133.4	135.7	148.2	149.6	147.5	180.2	208.9	238.2	
Households	131.0	151.1	175.5	200.5	230.0	265.2	296.9	313.5	
Other items (net)	-99.0	-67.9	-32.4	-13.2	31.6	118.4	175.9	306.3	
Of which:									
valuation changes	...	31.4	40.9	43.2	106.2	196.3	249.5	460.7	
Liabilities to nongovernment	405.9	422.1	459.3	511.5	559.6	635.4	653.5	732.4	
Broad money	397.7	410.5	432.3	480.8	524.7	582.0	593.7	665.6	
Currency in circulation	84.9	94.8	105.4	116.7	130.7	153.7	164.4	180.5	
Household deposits	167.6	185.5	203.9	225.4	252.8	261.3	284.2	273.3	
State enterprise deposits	142.6	126.6	117.7	137.1	135.0	158.9	138.7	174.8	
Private enterprise deposits	—	—	—	—	—	—	...	23.9	
Financial institutions' deposits 1/	2.6	3.6	5.3	1.6	6.2	8.1	6.4	13.1	
Bonds and savings notes	8.2	11.6	27.0	30.7	34.9	53.4	59.8	66.8	

(In percentage change, unless otherwise indicated)

Memorandum items:									
Credit									
Including other items		8.8	9.7	8.6	17.7	20.2	8.8	21.8	
Excluding other items		4.1	4.9	6.2	12.9	13.0	5.0	14.7	
Of which:									
State enterprises	...	2.7	5.7	9.1	12.1	6.2	-1.8	21.3	
Household sector	...	15.3	16.1	14.2	14.7	15.3	12.0	5.6	
General government (change in relation to GDP)	...	0.5	.0.1	0.3	5.4	4.1	0.5	3.2	
Broad money	...	3.2	5.3	11.2	9.1	10.9	2.0	12.1	
GDP growth	...	5.7	9.2	5.6	5.3	12.6	14.9	22.8	

Source: IMF Institute data base.

1/ Mainly State Development Bank.

Table 16. Hungary: Accounts of the National Bank of Hungary

(In billions of forint, end of period)

	1983	1984	1985	1986	1987	1988	1989	1990 Reference	Program
Net foreign assets	-340.5	-382.2	-411.6	-524.4	-677.0	-774.4	-954.3		
Foreign assets	91.0	121.3	172.7	159.8	138.3	138.6	162.7		
Less: Foreign liabilities	431.5	503.5	584.3	684.2	815.3	913.0	1117.0		
Domestic credit	664.7	671.4	741.7	876.6	990.4	1073.7	1312.4		
Central government (including State Development Bank) 1/	440.6	440.1	446.0	502.7	577.5	619.7	706.7		
Commercial banks 2/	--	--	--	--	253.8	225.4	252.1		
Other residents (net)	238.8	255.4	294.7	331.3	2.0	4.6	1.1		
Other items (net)	-14.7	-24.1	1.0	42.6	157.1	224.0	352.5		
Reserve money	324.2	289.2	330.1	352.2	313.4	299.3	358.1		

Source: IMF Institute data base.

1/ Note that this line closely approximates the sum of credits extended to the general government and to financial institutions in the monetary survey.

2/ Refinancing credits.

Table 17. Hungary: International Reserves and Other Foreign Assets

(In millions of U.S. dollars, end of period)

	1982	1983	1984	1985	1986	1987	1988	1989
International reserves in convertible currencies	941.9	1576.9	2026.1	2792.5	3053.0	2159.2	1976.3	1725.3
Gold 1/	213.4	367.9	504.7	639.9	750.6	525.1	509.7	479.1
Foreign exchange	728.5	1209.0	1521.4	2152.6	2302.4	1634.1	1466.6	1246.2
Nonconvertible currencies 2/	58.0	45.0	43.0	224.6	174.2	289.4	201.9	567.1
Total international reserves	999.9	1621.9	2069.1	3017.1	3227.2	2448.6	2178.2	2292.4
Other foreign assets								
Convertible currencies 3/	2007.3	2174.5	2408.2	3116.4	3185.9	3741.7	3659.9	3764.6
Nonconvertible currencies	395.2	430.0	384.0	422.1	481.0	523.5	501.7	669.0
Total international reserves and other foreign assets	3402.4	4226.4	4861.3	6555.6	6894.1	6713.8	6339.8	6726.0
Memorandum items:								
Change in convertible currency international reserves		635.0	449.2	766.4	260.5	-893.8	-182.9	-251.0
Change in nonconvertible international reserves		-13.0	-2.0	181.6	-50.4	115.2	-87.5	365.2

Source: IMF Institute data base.

1/ Actual holdings of gold, at national valuation of US$4275 per fine troy oune from 1982 to 1985, and US$4320 per troy ounce from 1986.

2/ Valued at the official exchange rates.

3/ Mainly trade credit extended by Hungarian enterprises.

Table 18. Hungary: Outstanding External Debt

(In millions of U.S. dollars, at end of period)

	1982	1983	1984	1985	1986	1987	1988	1989
Total external debt	11,515	12,125	12,216	15,106	17,928	20,531	20,150	20,966
In convertible currencies	10,216	10,746	10,983	13,955	16,907	19,584	19,603	20,605
By original maturity								
Short-term	3,261	3,904	2,977	3,019	3,494	3,103	3,363	3,306
Medium- and long-term	6,955	6,842	8,006	10,936	13,413	16,481	16,240	17,299
By type of credit:								
Financial loans	9,155	9,208	9,428	12,175	15,084	17,508	17,469	18,060
Trade-related credits	661	1,144	1,125	1,318	1,433	1,652	1,626	1,763
Intergovernment credits	5	4	3	2	1	0	--	--
Other	396	390	428	459	389	422	508	568
In nonconvertible currencies	1,299	1,379	1,233	1,151	1,021	947	547	361
By original maturity								
Short-term	250	367	916	106	111	184	120	87
Medium- and long-term	1,049	1,012	317	1,045	910	763	427	274
By type of credit:								
Financial loans	251	366	313	133	140	210	136	88
Trade-related credits	39	30	24	0	--	--	--	--
Intergovernment credits	974	948	863	1,009	873	728	438	260
Other	35	38	32	8	8	8	8	12
Memorandum item:								
Convertible currency debt 1/								
(as percent of GDP)	44.1	51.1	53.9	67.7	71.2	75.0	70.1	70.3

Source: IMF Institute data base

1/ End of period convertible currency external debt divided by GDP for the year as a whole in local currency units and converted into U.S. Dollars at the period average forint/U.S. Dollar exchange rate.

Table 19. Hungary: External Debt Service in Convertible Currencies

	1982	1983	1984	1985	1986	1987	1988	1989
	(In millions of U.S. dollars)							
Total debt service	2,432	2,351	2,705	3,689	4,182	3,747	3,510	3,569
a. Principal	1235	1496	1761	2670	2967	2524	2204	1964
Excluding Fund repurchases	1,235	1,496	1,761	2,580	2,919	2,170	1,849	1,740
Fund repurchases	0	0	0	90	48	354	355	224
b. Interest	1,197	855	944	1,019	1,215	1,223	1,306	1,605
	(In percent)							
Total debt service 1/	47.0	45.4	51.0	79.2	87.1	64.2	54.8	48.2
a. Principal								
Excluding Fund repurchases	23.9	28.9	33.2	55.4	60.8	37.2	28.9	23.5
Fund repurchases	0.0	0.0	0.0	1.9	1.0	6.1	5.5	3.0
b. Interest	23.1	16.5	17.8	21.9	25.3	20.9	20.4	21.7

Sources: IMF Institute data base.

1/ As percent of merchandise exports, and travel and income credits.

Table 20. Hungary: Commodity Composition of Nonruble Trade 1/

(In millions of U.S. dollars)

	1986	1987	1988	1989
Exports				
Energy products	137.9	150.0	186.4	202.8
Raw materials and semifinished products	1639.3	1930.7	2413.0	2671.3
Capital goods and transportation equipment	608.9	610.8	727.0	626.8
Industrial consumer goods	687.4	822.3	899.2	897.9
Food products	1129.8	1194.4	1475.1	1618.4
Total	4203.3	4708.2	5700.7	6017.2
Of which: Nonenergy	4065.4	4558.2	5514.3	5814.5
Imports				
Energy products	213.8	148.9	84.0	40.1
Raw materials and semifinished products	2683.8	2968.5	3282.5	3281.6
Capital goods and transportation equipment	658.1	751.3	716.2	943.6
Industrial consumer goods	583.5	615.7	534.1	645.0
Food products	532.8	543.4	565.0	552.5
Total	4672.0	5027.8	5181.8	5462.8
Of which: Nonenergy	4458.2	4878.9	5097.8	5422.7
Balance of trade				
Energy products	−75.8	1.0	102.4	162.7
Raw materials and semifinished products	−1044.5	−1037.7	−869.5	−610.3
Capital goods and transportation equipment	−49.2	−140.6	10.8	−316.8
Industrial consumer goods	103.9	206.6	365.0	252.9
Food products	597.0	650.9	910.1	1065.9
Total	−468.6	−319.8	518.8	554.4
Of which: Nonenergy	−392.8	−320.7	416.5	391.8

Source: IMF Institute data base.

1/ Exports are on an f.o.b. basis, imports on a c.i.f. basis.

Table 21. Hungary: Balance of Payments in Nonconvertible Currencies

(In millions of U.S. dollars)

	1982	1983	1984	1985	1986	1987	1988	1989	1990 Estimate
Trade balance	-258.0	-339.0	-111.0	320.0	17.0	43.0	94.0	507.0	194.0
Exports	4207.0	4146.0	4174.0	4390.0	5012.0	4916.0	4484.0	4047.0	2746.0
Imports	-4465.0	-4485.0	-4285.0	-4070.0	-4995.0	-4873.0	-4390.0	-3540.0	-2552.0
Services (net)	21.0	85.0	82.0	67.0	112.0	157.0	136.0	355.0	7.0
Freight and insurance, net	-91.0	-70.0	-65.0	-83.0	-76.0	-82.0	-77.0	-56.0	-10.0
Travel (net)	81.0	96.0	104.0	112.0	167.0	170.0	113.0	190.0	52.0
Credits	138.0	158.0	167.0	177.0	239.0	254.0	195.0	246.0	160.0
Debits	-57.0	-62.0	-63.0	-65.0	-72.0	-84.0	-82.0	-56.0	-108.0
Investment income (net)	5.0	-17.0	-34.0	-34.0	-28.0	-39.0	-16.0	-7.0	17.0
Credits	30.0	20.0	11.0	9.0	9.0	12.0	10.0	13.0	34.0
Debits	-25.0	-37.0	-45.0	-43.0	-37.0	-51.0	-26.0	-20.0	-17.0
Other current payments (net)	26.0	76.0	77.0	72.0	49.0	108.0	116.0	228.0	-52.0
Unrequited transfers (net)	2.0	3.0	3.0	4.0	4.0	3.0	2.0	4.0	53.0
Current account	-235.0	-251.0	-26.0	391.0	133.0	203.0	232.0	866.0	254.0
Medium– and long–term capital	96.0	100.0	15.0	-3.0	-215.0	-177.0	-268.0	-278.0	-98.0
Assets (net)	-18.0	8.0	-5.0	15.0	-48.0	-69.0	-69.0	-127.0	25.0
Liabilities (net)	114.0	92.0	20.0	-18.0	-167.0	-108.0	-199.0	-151.0	-123.0
Disbursements	133.0	131.0	182.0	54.0	66.0	59.0	44.0	20.0	12.0
Amortization	-19.0	-39.0	-162.0	-72.0	-233.0	-167.0	-243.0	-170.0	-135.0
Short–term capital (including errors and omissions)	180.0	128.0	3.0	-206.4	31.6	89.2	-51.5	-222.8	79.9
Capital account	276.0	238.0	24.0	-209.4	-183.4	-87.8	-319.5	-500.8	-18.1
Overall balance	41.0	-13.0	-2.0	181.6	-50.4	115.2	-87.5	365.2	235.9
Financing	-41.0	13.0	2.0	-181.6	50.4	-115.2	87.5	-365.2	-235.9
Change in reserves (inc.=–)	-40.0	13.0	2.0	-181.6	50.4	-115.2	87.5	-365.2	-235.9

Sources: IMF Institute data base

Table 22. Hungary: Ruble Trade, Customs Basis

(In millions of U.S. dollars and percentage change)

	1984	1985	1986	1987	1988	1989	1990
Exports, fob	3685.9	4025.2	4675.5	4559.6	4124.8	3653.0	2517.0
(percent change)		9.2	16.2	−2.5	−9.5	−11.4	−31.1
Exports fob, 1986 prices	4323.3	4680.5	4675.5	4792.0	4820.5	4169.0	2775.4
(percent change)		8.3	−0.1	2.5	0.6	−13.5	−33.4
Export prices, 1986=100	85.3	86.0	100.0	95.2	85.6	87.6	90.7
(percent change)		0.9	16.3	−4.9	−10.1	2.4	3.5
Imports, cif	3805.5	3849.8	4654.7	4462.1	4040.4	3397.0	2518.0
(percent change)		1.2	20.9	−4.1	−9.5	−15.9	−25.9
Imports, cif, 1986 prices	4500.9	4484.2	4654.7	4826.5	5021.7	4163.7	3080.2
(percent change)		−0.4	3.8	3.7	4.0	−17.1	−26.0
Import prices, 1986=100	84.5	85.9	100.0	92.5	80.5	81.6	81.7
(percent change)		1.5	16.5	−7.6	−13.0	1.4	0.2
Terms of trade	100.8	100.2	100.0	102.9	106.3	107.4	110.9
(percent change)		−0.7	−0.2	2.9	3.3	1.0	3.3

Source: IMF Institute data base.

Table 23. Hungary: Commodity Composition of Ruble Trade 1/

	1986	1987	1988	1989
Exports				
Energy products	26.1	21.5	14.9	15.3
Raw materials and semifinished products	1041.6	997.1	893.4	852.7
Capital goods and transportation equipment	2147.3	2127.0	1922.3	1693.6
Industrial consumer goods	779.5	741.9	679.8	617.4
Food products	665.1	614.5	554.9	476.4
Total	4659.6	4502.0	4065.3	3655.4
Of which: Nonenergy	4633.4	4480.4	4050.3	3640.1
Imports				
Energy products	1489.2	1286.0	1101.6	934.6
Raw materials and semifinished products	1514.1	1486.9	1399.5	1200.8
Capital goods and transportation equipment	944.8	944.8	810.9	658.4
Industrial consumer goods	522.8	568.0	545.6	523.6
Food products	130.1	138.1	103.1	82.8
Total	4601.0	4423.8	3960.7	3400.2
Of which: Nonenergy	3111.8	3137.9	2859.0	2465.6
Balance of trade				
Energy products	−1463.1	−1264.5	−1086.7	−919.4
Raw materials and semifinished products	−472.6	−489.8	−506.1	−348.1
Capital goods and transportation equipment	1202.5	1182.1	1111.4	1035.2
Industrial consumer goods	256.7	173.8	134.2	93.8
Food products	535.0	476.4	451.8	393.6
Total	58.5	78.0	104.6	255.1
Of which: Nonenergy	1521.6	1342.5	1191.3	1174.5

Source: IMF Institute data base.

1/ Exports are on a f.o.b. basis and imports on a c.i.f. basis. Trade flows settled in rubles are converted from their forint value given in official statistics at the period U.S. dollar exchange rate.

III. Introduction to Financial Programming

Nature of Financial Programming

A *financial program* is a comprehensive set of policy measures designed to achieve a given set of macroeconomic goals. These goals could simply be to maintain a given level of economic performance. More often, however, the policies are designed to eliminate disequilibrium between aggregate domestic demand and supply, which typically manifests itself in balance of payments problems, rising inflation, and low output growth.

The term "financial program" is commonly used to describe adjustment programs which support use of Fund resources, but may also be applied in the absence of a Fund arrangement. It emphasizes the importance of monetary, fiscal, and exchange rate policies in controlling domestic demand and correcting balance of payments disequilibria. In addition—as a practical consideration—financial data to monitor the implementation of such policies are typically available on a more timely basis than other economic data. However, it should be underscored that financial programs also incorporate the effects of other policy instruments, most prominently those aimed at increasing aggregate supply.

Where macroeconomic imbalances exist, some form of correction (or *adjustment*) will ultimately be necessary in order to bring claims on resources in line with those available. If deliberate policy actions are not taken, the adjustment is likely to be disorderly and inefficient. For example, reserves may be depleted and creditors may become unwilling to lend further to a country. A drastic cut in imports could ensue, with consequent negative effects on economic growth and welfare. The distinguishing feature of a financial program is that it seeks to achieve an *orderly adjustment*, through the early adoption of corrective policy measures, and through the provision of appropriate amounts of external financing. This should minimize losses in output and employment during the adjustment period while eventually leading to a balance of payments position that is sustainable.

Sustainability of the balance of payments may be assessed with reference to the evolution of the external current account balance over the medium term. While circumstances may vary from one country to another, in general terms it may be said that a sustainable current account position is one that can be financed on a lasting basis with the expected capital inflows and which, at the same time, is consistent with adequate growth, price stability, and the country's ability to service fully its external debt servicing obligations.

A financial program thus needs to be set in a *forward looking time framework*. The concept of medium-term is not a rigid one; medium-term scenarios have generally considered a time horizon of at least five years. Typically, programs for the forthcoming year are worked out in considerable detail because of the more imminent need to formulate a comprehensive package of policy measures and the more readily available and reliable information. Forecasts of the more distant years are less detailed, often focusing on the broad implications for external adjustment, and are by their nature less certain.

A Basic Financial Programming Framework 1/

An integrated system of macroeconomic accounts, as described in Chapter II, covering national income and expenditure, as well as financial flows and associated stocks, is essential in the construction of financial programs. These accounts provide the information needed to assess the performance of the economy and the need for policy adjustment. They also provide a framework and consistency checks for policy analysis. The accounting relationships in the framework highlight the fact that any sector's spending beyond its income must be financed by the savings of other sectors, and that such excess spending by an entire economy is possible only when financed from external sources.

To be of interest to policy makers, the accounting framework must be complemented by the specification of a set of *behavioral relationships*. These relations indicate the typical reaction or response of some of the variables included in the accounting framework to changes in other variables. These *behavioral relationships* together with the *accounting identities* form a schematic quantitative representation, or "model", of the relevant economic processes. This framework can be used to assess the changes in *policy variables*, i.e., variables that are under the authorities' control, needed to achieve given policy *objectives* for such variables as inflation and the balance of payments, which are endogenously determined.

The design of programs is subject to many uncertainties and difficulties. Behavioral relationships may be difficult to identify and estimate with any precision and they may vary across countries and over time depending on institutional, political, and other factors. Moreover, when major policy shifts and structural reforms are being undertaken, behavior in the post-reform period may differ greatly from historical patterns. Analysis may be further complicated by problems of assessing the timing of policy effects, the impact of expectations on behavioral responses, and the interrelations among measures in complex policy packages. Finally, assumed changes in *exogenous* variables, which are determined independently of the processes illustrated in the model, may prove to be incorrect.

1/ A more detailed review of a framework for financial programming can be found in "Theoretical Aspects of the Design of Fund-Supported Adjustment Programs," IMF, Occasional Paper No.55, September 1987.

Policy Content of Programs

Discussion of the policy options can be framed around two accounting identities discussed in Chapter II. Specifically:

$$GDI - A = CA \qquad (1)$$

and

$$CA + \Delta FI = \Delta R \qquad (2)$$

where:

GDI	=	gross national disposable income
A	=	domestic absorption, i.e., residents' expenditure on domestic and foreign goods and services
CA	=	external current account balance
ΔFI	=	net capital inflows
ΔR	=	the change in net official international reserves

Equation (1) indicates that an improvement in the external current account balance requires either an increase in a country's output or a reduction in its expenditure. Accordingly, adjustment policies may aim to increase output and reduce domestic expenditure to allow a greater proportion of output to be devoted to exports and a lower proportion of expenditures to imports.

Equation (2) is the balance of payments identity: any excess of absorption over income, as reflected in a current account deficit, must be financed either by capital inflows or a drawdown of reserves.

1. Demand management policies

Demand management policies primarily aim at reducing domestic demand (or absorption) when an external current account deficit and/or inflationary pressures need to be reduced. These primarily comprise *monetary*, *fiscal* and *incomes* policies, but other measures such as an exchange rate devaluation may also include expenditure reducing elements.

In many instances the source of excess domestic demand is the *fiscal sector*. A combination of a reduction in public sector outlays and an increase in revenues may be called for. However, simple measures of the government's overall balance may not give adequate indication of the demand effects of fiscal policy. In particular, how the overall balance is financed is important in determining program impact.

Domestic absorption can also be dampened by restraining *monetary aggregates*—for example, by introducing measures to change the volume of credit extended to the private sector and/or the public sector. Monetary and fiscal policies are linked to the extent that the banking system provides net financing (whether positive or negative) to the public sector. For example, a narrowing of the public sector deficit that reduces the need for bank financing (or increases recourse to nonbank financing of a given deficit) will directly affect the balance sheet of the banking system. Other things being equal, this would result in a decline in monetary aggregates.

2. Expenditure-switching policies

Many programs seek to complement reductions in absorption by expenditure-switching measures and, in particular, *exchange rate policy*. By changing the relative price of foreign and domestic goods facing both residents and nonresidents—i.e., from a resident's perspective, increasing the price of a country's exports and imports relative to the price of domestic goods—an exchange rate devaluation aims to: (1) increase the global demand for domestic goods and services while reducing residents' domestic absorption by discouraging imports, and (2) from the supply side, raise incentives to produce goods for export or that compete with imports. By redirecting output from domestic absorption to the external sector, the negative effects of demand restraint on output can be minimized.

Other examples of expenditure-switching policies include removal of price controls and quantitative trade restrictions.

3. Structural policies

Structural policies aim at the enhancement of supply to close the absorption-output gap. These may be broadly divided into: (1) policies designed to raise output from existing resources through increased allocative efficiency; and (2) policies to expand the productive capacity of the economy. While in practice it is difficult to distinguish policies serving these two purposes, conceptually one can think of the former category including all measures to reduce the distortions that drive a wedge between prices and marginal cost. Such distortions can arise, for example, from price controls, imperfect competition, taxes and subsidies, and trade and exchange restrictions.

Increases in capacity require policies that encourage investment and savings. Examples include maintaining realistic interest rates, reducing fiscal deficits, reallocating fiscal expenditures toward activity with the strongest benefits for growth and economic development, and policies that tend to guide new resources to investments with the highest rates of return. By their nature, substantial time may be needed for structural policies to show results.

4. Financing options

The ability to attract capital inflows to sustain an external current account deficit without running into debt service problems depends, among other things, on the judgement of creditors as to the creditworthiness of the country and how efficiently the borrowed funds are used. In particular, if foreign borrowing is used to finance investments which generate sufficient returns to finance the repayment of such funds, then debt servicing problems should not arise. Debt servicing problems, however, may be expected when resources are used inefficiently or to support domestic consumption only. In addition, changes in world economic conditions may significantly affect the availability and affordability of funds. For example, rising interest rates in the early 1980s exacerbated the debt servicing difficulties experienced by many developing countries.

Considerations relating to *external debt management* have become an increasingly important part of program design. Key debt relationships need to be monitored on a medium-term basis, under alternative assumptions about the country's own policies and the behavior of the external environment, including interest rates. Development of such medium-term scenarios has represented an important aspect of the Fund's work in stabilization programs.

Financing may also take the form of a *reduction in international reserves*. However such possibilities are limited by the size of the initial stock of reserves.

In addition to the above sources of *voluntary* external financing, in extreme circumstances some countries may finance external deficits by accumulating *arrears*. Arrears, however, constitute payment restrictions and are therefore contrary to Fund policies. In addition, they undermine creditor confidence and, therefore, complicate relations with external creditors.

★ ★ ★ ★

Policies, to be effective, need to be constructed and implemented in a *mutually supportive* manner. For example, a depreciation of the exchange rate, if not supported by demand restraint, may fail to redirect resources to the external sector while raising the inflationary pressures in the economy.

In designing the objectives of a policy package, account should be taken of *trade-offs* between different objectives and, thus, of the policies needed to achieve them. Listed below are several examples. A depreciation of the exchange rate, aimed at reducing the external current account deficit, will also raise the domestic currency costs of servicing the external debt. In the absence of other measures, this will raise the fiscal deficit. Policies aimed at sharply reducing inflation may not be consistent with strong output growth in the short-run, particularly if prices are not fully flexible downward. Balance of payments surpluses may result in excessive monetary growth and inflationary pressures. Supply side measures to liberalize trade may result in an initial deterioration in the overall balance of payments position as the pent up demand for imports is unleashed; the removal of price controls is likely to raise inflation, at least initially.

Steps in Economic Forecasting

Preparation of a financial program requires an assessment of economic problems and the quantification of a coordinated set of policy instruments to achieve a given outcome. It requires completion of the major sector accounts to provide an internally consistent, and feasible, scenario of developments that could result from adopting a given package of policy measures. Given the linkages among the accounts, an iterative, rather than sequential, procedure is likely to be required to ensure a consistent program.

The workshop series is developed by sector, with the intention of providing participants with an understanding of the issues and methods needed for forecasting individual sectors. However, while the focus at any point in time will be on a particular sector, the overall aim is to develop a consistent macroeconomic projection of the Hungarian economy in 1990, and its implications for the medium-term balance of payments position. A first step is the development of the so-called the *reference scenario*, broadly based on the assumption that policies remain unchanged from the recent past. The reference scenario is intended to indicate whether the existing problems are likely to be resolved by themselves, to remain the same, or even worsen.

An assessment of what constitutes an unchanged policy stance involves elements of judgement. For example, if budgeted expenditures have regularly been overrun by wide margins, then continuation of this practice could be considered to constitute one element of an unchanged policy stance. Similarly, if the exchange rate has been adjusted according to the differential between domestic and trading partners' inflation rates, then adoption of this rule could be another element of unchanged policies. In assessing the policy stance, it is important that the coverage be comprehensive, including fiscal, monetary (including interest rate), exchange rate, and structural issues.

Reference scenarios may differ for a variety of reasons. These may include differences in the relative importance attached to the various economic problems; in interpretation of what constitutes an unchanged policy stance; in assessment of the policy trade-offs; and in the methods used in forecasting. While formulation of these scenarios necessarily involves a considerable element of judgement, it needs to be underscored that repeated cross-checking of sectoral forecasts is required to ensure overall *behavioral* and *accounting* consistency.

The reference scenario, serves as a benchmark for elaborating a normative *program scenario*. This scenario would be based on an explicit policy package designed to achieve a *desired* set of objectives. Comparison of reference and program scenarios would indicate the expected impact of the policy package.

Below are some suggested general guidelines for preparing a financial program. The more technical details are treated separately in the individual workshops.

1. Evaluate economic problems

An understanding of the economic, institutional and socio/political *structure* of the economy and *recent economic developments* is essential for forecasting and policy analysis. The type of *policy instruments* available should also be identified. A diagnosis should be made regarding:

(1) the *nature* of the economic imbalance. If the problem is expected to be short-lived (cyclical, seasonal, etc.) all that may be required is some bridge financing or a temporary drawdown of reserves. More permanent imbalances will likely need to rely more heavily on a package of adjustment measures.

(2) the *source* of the imbalance. If at root of the problem is a large fiscal deficit, corrective measures will need to be implemented in this area. If the cause is *external*, for example a terms of trade deterioration, an exchange rate adjustment is more likely to be considered as part of a package to improve current account prospects.

(3) the *seriousness* of the imbalance related to, among other things, the dimensions of the problem and availability of financing. The more urgently the imbalances need to be addressed, the more drastic adjustment measures that will be needed.

2. Identify developments that are outside the authorities' control

External sector forecasts involve interrelationships with the rest of the world and must, therefore, take account of developments in the world economy, including prospects for commodity and other foreign trade prices, world interest rates, and output and demand growth in partner and competitor countries. Forecasts of these variables can be obtained from various private, government, and international trade organizations. Chapter V on balance of payments forecasting summarizes forecasts in the Fund's World Economic Outlook that may be of relevance when making projections for the Hungarian economy. Nevertheless, a considerable degree of uncertainty must underlie these forecasts. It is thus useful to undertake sensitivity analyses of the effects of deviations from projected levels of some of the more important external variables.

3. Set preliminary targets and develop policy package

The differences between the reference scenario and the program scenario should be noted. In a reference scenario, the preliminary targets are derived as an *outcome* of the assumption of a continuation of the existing policies. By contrast, in a program scenario targets are first *set* and then policy measures are adopted to meet these targets. The outcome of the reference scenario should provide a basis for establishing appropriate targets for the program scenario.

Targets are typically set for the balance of payments—in terms of the current account balance and/or the level of international reserves—prices, and output. They should be consistent with a viable balance of payments position, in the medium term, as well as with growth and inflation objectives.

4. Prepare sectoral forecasts

Given the iterative nature of the exercise, there are many possible approaches and starting points in developing a scenario. The approach taken in the forthcoming workshops is to start with a preliminary price and output projection, followed by forecasts for the balance of payments, fiscal sector and finally the monetary sector. However, at various stages there will be a need to iterate among the sectoral forecasts to ensure accounting and behavioral consistency and the feasibility of achieving the stated targets. This is highlighted by the following examples.

Assume that a preliminary set of projections or targets has been made for prices, real output, and the change in net international reserves. The implications of these projections for the external sector can be verified by forecasting values for exports and capital flows and deriving imports residually. However, in a second round the derived import figure must be made consistent with the demand for imports at the projected level of nominal output (a behavioral relationship). If, for instance, the demand for imports is greater than the value of imports derived residually, some adjustment must be made. The basic choices include:

(1) increasing the foreign exchange available to support a higher level of imports, either by adopting policies to raise export receipts or by seeking out additional financing;

(2) lowering the initial projection or target for net international reserves to allow for a higher level of imports;

(3) reducing the initial projection or target for nominal output to lower the demand for imports; and

(4) a combination of some of the above.

A similar iterative procedure would be carried out for the fiscal and monetary sectors. For instance, projections for prices, output, and net foreign assets underlie any estimate of net banking system domestic credit. If the implied bank credit extended to the government sector is insufficient to cover the estimated fiscal deficit then the following options are available:

(1) introduce a package of fiscal measures to reduce the public sector deficit, which may result in lower nominal output growth;

(2) redirect credit from the private sector to the government sector, which may also have a dampening effect on nominal output growth;

(3) raise additional external financing, which has obvious balance of payments implications;

(4) increase nonbank domestic financing, which may have interest rate implications;

(5) increase bank credit extended to the government, accepting the likely negative effects on inflation and/or the balance of payments; and

(6) a combination of some of the above.

In general, abstracting from some of the peculiarities and discrepancies evident in any data set—some of which were discussed in Chapter II for the case of Hungary—the following accounting relations should hold:

• output from the expenditure side should be based on fiscal data for government consumption and investment and on external data for net foreign expenditure;

• government recourse to banking system credit, as shown in the fiscal data, should be consistent with the change in net domestic credit to the government, as reported in the monetary accounts; and

• government recourse to external financing, as shown in the fiscal data, and changes in the net foreign asset position in the balance sheet of the banking system should have counterpart entries in the capital flows of the balance of payments.

Key behavioral relationships that need to be considered include:

• the demand for money and its relationship to nominal output and other variables

• the demand for imports and its relationship to nominal output and other variables

• the relationship between private sector bank credit and private investment and imports

5. Review desirability of use of Fund resources

This step is relevant for the program scenario. A decision that a program should be supported by use of Fund resources requires that *performance criteria* be set. Performance criteria provide a direct link between program implementation and the disbursement of the Fund's resources. Failure to observe the performance criteria results in interruption of the member's drawings under an arrangement. Depending on the causes and nature of the deviations, either a waiver, or modification, may be granted to permit a resumption of drawings, or a new understanding may need to be reached.

Performance criteria and other monitoring devices are intended to be limited to those necessary to evaluate implementation of the program so as to avoid excessive involvement of the Fund in the details of economic policy making.

The following are the most commonly used types of performance criteria:

- a ceiling on domestic bank credit expansion;

- a sub-ceiling on net domestic bank credit to the government, or the nonfinancial public sector;

- ceilings on nonconsessional external borrowing, including short and medium-and long-term debts;

- a floor on net international reserves; and

- understandings that there will not be new, or an intensification of existing, exchange and import restrictions.

Bank credit ceilings may be set at either the level of the monetary survey or the monetary authorities' accounts. The former provides immediate consistency with targets (through the inflation and growth rate used in predicting the demand for money and the change in net foreign assets), but leaves open the measures the authorities may take to limit monetary aggregates. Placement of the ceilings at the level of the monetary authorities' accounts has the advantage of dealing with aggregates more subject to the authorities' control, but means that consistency with targets depends on the stability of the assumed money supply function.

Other kinds of policies may, where appropriate, also be subject to performance criteria. Important in this context have been additional understandings affecting the exchange and trade system, including measures relating to exchange rate policy and to the reduction or elimination of external payments arrears.

Disbursements of Fund monies can also be subject to completion of a *review*, which typically monitors structural and other policies that may not be amenable to quantitative performance criteria.

Prior actions, i.e., implementation of policy measures seen as critical to the effectiveness of an adjustment program prior to approval of a Fund arrangement, may also be required. Such actions are particularly important where severe imbalances exist, or in cases where the record of policy implementation has been weak.

Issues for Discussion

1. On the basis of Chapters I and II, discuss the main economic problems facing Hungary at end-1989. This review should identify the main macroeconomic and structural weaknesses and provide some initial assessment of the causes, size, and urgency of the economic difficulties.

2. Assess the policy stance of the authorities' in the recent past. Consider the effectiveness of these policies in achieving major economic objectives. Identify the policy instruments available to the authorities.

3. Review in broad terms the main assumptions that will underlie the reference scenario.

4. What are the major factors affecting economic performance that you consider to be outside of the authorities' control?

IV. Prices, Output, and Expenditure

This workshop reviews techniques for projecting inflation, output, and the composition of expenditure in Hungary in 1990. Such forecasts are central to a stabilization program since inflation and growth are usually among the major goals of policy. Similarly, the composition of expenditure affects the growth potential and the external balance of the economy.

Prices

1. Introduction

In 1989, 63 percent (compared with 56 percent in 1985) of consumer goods had *free* prices, i.e., prices were subject to only the general rule that they not exceed the domestic price of comparable imports. A further 20 percent of consumer goods prices were subject to a requirement of *advance reporting* or *prior consultation* with the authorities. The remaining 17 percent of prices were subject to a maximum limit (compared with 44 percent in 1985).

Repeated efforts to overhaul the price system through administrative price realignments, the linkage of raw-materials and energy prices to world market prices, and the adoption of rules to allow for greater flexibility in the pricing policy of enterprises, avoided the accumulation of major distortions in relative prices that characterized most centrally planned economies. Nevertheless, the adjustment of prices to market conditions was hampered by three main factors. First, the pricing rules and the close monitoring of free price formation were used as an important instrument of anti-inflationary policy. Second, ad hoc taxes and subsidies were used extensively to affect individual enterprise results: current government subsidies and transfers accounted for about one third of GDP in 1989, a proportion that changed little in the 1980s. Finally, Hungarian industry was characterized by a very high degree of concentration and little competition. This stemmed from the early days of central planning when agreements among enterprises in a branch of industry would subdivide the product range into a number of distinct items or groups, each to be produced by one or a few firms. Not only were production units designed to be large and to take advantage of economies of scale, but they developed the in-house capacity to produce certain essential inputs, in light of uncertain external supplies, rather than relying on smaller-scale suppliers of producer goods as in a typical market economy. Competition was also impeded by the traditional reliance on foreign trade controls.

2. Forecasting inflation

a. General considerations

Forecasting inflation involves an assessment of many different factors, some of which are listed below:

(1)   What are the *cost pressures* tending to increase prices? An example of a major *cost-push* (or supply side) effect on prices was the steep rise in world energy prices in 1973–74 and 1979–80. In estimating cost pressures, an assessment needs to be made regarding the proportion of the increase in costs that will be passed onto prices rather than being absorbed by enterprises in the form of lower profits. This will depend importantly on the stance of economic policies (point 2 below) and the degree of competition among enterprises. Enterprises response to cost increases will also depend on the willingness of the government to extend *tax concessions* and/or *subsidies* to those sectors experiencing cost increases.

(2)   What is the stance of *economic policies* and how has it changed from the previous year? For example, an easing of monetary policy is likely to put upward pressures on prices, especially if real output remains unchanged, as residents attempt to spend increased money balances on goods and services (*demand-pull* inflation).

(3)   Does a change in one, or a few, prices constitute a change in the *overall price level* or does it reflect a change in *relative prices* that should be offset by changes in the opposite direction in other prices? *Relative price* changes act as a signal to redirect scarce resources to activities where they can be most productively used. By contrast, increases in the *overall price* level normally indicate the existence of excess demand pressures in the economy. In practice, the distinction is blurred because of a downward rigidity of prices in the short-run. Relative price changes are, thus, typically also reflected in upward adjustments in the overall price level, at least temporarily.

(4)   How do people's *expectations* about future movements in the price level affect today's increase in the price level? While modeling expectations has generated considerable debate and empirical work, the underlying notion is relatively simple: people's behavior today will be affected by how they perceive the future.

(5)   The *institutional arrangements* in a country can also affect price developments. These include price control arrangements, competition policy, and the foreign trade system. The more liberal the latter, the greater the proportion of any excess demand that is likely to be dissipated through the balance of payments rather than in domestic price increases. Equally, price behavior may be strongly influenced by the exchange rate regime: the less flexible is the exchange rate system, the more the demand pressures will be reflected in a drawdown of foreign exchange reserves rather than in an increase in prices.

b.   A practical approach

The approach described below is designed to provide the outlines of a possible methodology for estimating inflation based on a *cost-approach*. The estimates of cost increases can only be approximations since over time they could have wider ripple effects as they work themselves throughout the economy. Similarly, price changes observed in any given period may reflect not only changes in cost pressures in that period but also the continuing effects of cost changes from previous periods. For example, the impact of an increase in import prices may at first only be felt on the prices of goods imported directly and domestic goods using imported inputs. However, over time, other domestically produced goods are also likely to face higher input costs as these increases spread through the economy. This effect will be more pronounced if wages are raised to compensate for price increases.

Once some benchmark estimate is derived, it must be adjusted to take account of the *stance of economic policies*. For example, a tightening of policies is likely to be reflected in less of a pass-through of costs into prices as demand conditions weaken and, possibly, wages and prices show more downward flexibility. By contrast, a loosening of policies is likely to magnify the ripple effects of the cost-push pressures. Such adjustments are by their nature judgmental. Nevertheless, a more accurate picture of the stance of economic policies is likely to emerge on completion of forecasts of the fiscal and monetary accounts (Chapters VI and VII). This may require a revision to the initial estimates for inflation calculated in this workshop.

The two indices that this exercise focuses on are the consumer price index (CPI) and the deflator for gross domestic product (PGDP). The CPI is an index of prices of a typical basket of imported and domestically produced goods that are *consumed* by residents. The PGDP, by contrast, is a price index for all goods *produced*, both for the home market and for export. Differences in movements in the CPI and PGDP would thus be expected to reflect, among other things, differences in the movements of export and import prices. For example, if import prices were to increase by much more than export prices, other things being equal, inflation, as measured by the CPI, would be expected to be higher than as shown by the PGDP.

It should, however, be noted that in reality the separation of the effect of import prices on the CPI and of export prices on the PGDP is not clear cut. The ripple effect of an increase in import prices on domestically produced goods, and thus on the PGDP, has already been discussed. As regards an increase in export prices, some exportable products may be consumed domestically. To the extent that enterprises ask the same price of these products, whether they are exported or sold at home, the effect of changes in export prices could have a direct impact on the CPI.

Based on the underlying cost pressures in the economy, Table 1 projects inflation for 1989, for both the CPI and PGDP. Actual data available on an ex-post basis is used. Table 2 is a working sheet summarizing the calculations underlying the various cost components of Table 1.

The starting point is to assume that, in the absence of changes in cost pressures, inflation will remain at about its 1988 rate (line 1, Table 1). In 1989 there were at least three factors that should have worked in the direction of moderating inflation:

Table 1. Hungary: Estimates of Inflation for 1989 Based on Cost Factors

(percentage change)

	CPI	PGDP
(1) Inflation in 1988	15.7	15.2
Cost effects in 1989 of:		
(2) nonrecurrent impact of 1988 value added tax	−7.0	−7.0
(3) wage moderation	−2.3	−2.3
(4) smaller reduction in subsidies	−0.7	−0.7
(5) import price changes	5.7	3.0
(6) export price changes	1.0	6.5
(7) interest rate changes	2.2	2.2
(8) estimated inflation in 1989 from cost-side	14.6	16.9
(1)+(2)+(3)+(4)+(5)+(6)+(7)		
Memorandum item:		
Actual inflation in 1989	17.0	18.7

Source: IMF Institute data base; see also Table 2 for calculations underlying the above figures.

(1) The introduction of a value-added tax in 1988 is estimated to have led to a once-and-for-all jump in the price level in that year equivalent to about 7.0 percentage points (line 2, Table 1).

(2) Despite the fact that wage increases in the socialized sector exceeded those planned by wide margins—19 percent compared to a plan of 6 percent—wages in 1989 still rose by about 5 percentage points less than in 1988. The large wage awards of 1988 reflected the grossing up of incomes prior to the introduction of the personal income tax so as to preserve the net income of employees. With the wage bill equivalent to about one-third of the value of output, this moderation in wage growth could be expected to lower inflation by about 2 percentage points (line 3 of Table 1 and calculation 1 of Table 2).

CALCULATION 1
Wage Moderation (line 3 of Table 1)

	1987	1988	1989
Socialized sector wage bill			
(in billions of forint)	425.2	530.6	629.1
(percentage change)	...	24.8	18.6

$$\frac{\text{wage bill}}{\text{GDP}} \mid 1988 \times (18.6 - 24.8)$$

$$= \frac{530.6}{1408.8} \times -6.2$$

$$= -2.3\%$$

CALCULATION 2
Smaller Reduction in Subsidies (line 4 of Table 1)

	1987	1988	1989
General government subsidies			
(in billions of forint)	199.2	196.7	216.4
(percent of GDP)	16.2	14.0	12.5
Reduction in subsidies			
(in percentage points of GDP)		-2.2	-1.5

Calculation:

1.5 - 2.2 = -0.7

CALCULATION 3
External Prices (lines 5 and 6 of Table 1)

	1988	1989
	(Percentage change)	
a. import prices (in US$)	-3.5	1.4
b. export prices (in US$)	-0.5	2.6
c. exchange rate (forint/US$)	7.3	17.2
d. import prices (in forint)	3.5	18.8
e. export prices (in forint)	6.8	20.2

$$\frac{\text{imports}}{\text{GDP}} \mid 1988 \times (18.8 - 3.5)$$

$$= \frac{527.5}{1408.8} \times 15.3$$

$$= 5.7\%$$

$$\frac{\text{exports}}{\text{GDP}} \mid 1988 \times (20.2 - 6.8)$$

$$= \frac{574.0}{1408.8} \times 13.4$$

$$= 5.5\%$$

CALCULATION 4
Interest Rate (line 8 of Table 1)

	1987	1988	1989
Interest rates for enterprises			
(less than one year)			
Credits	13.0	18.3	23.0
Deposits	6.0	14.2	19.0

Interest cost
(Percentage change)

43.6
36.8
...

Calculation:

1989 (702.6 x .23) - (187.9 x .19) = 125.9
1988 (591.7 x .183) - (145.1 x .142) = 87.7
1987 (570.1 x .13) - (167.0 x .06) = 64.1

$$\frac{\text{net credits outstanding}}{\text{GDP}} \mid 1988 \times (43.6 - 36.8)$$

$$= \frac{446.6}{1408.8} \times 6.8 = 2.2$$

Source: Staff estimates.

(3)   Government subsidies, in relation to GDP, fell by 0.7 percentage points less in 1989 than in 1988, which should have moderated pressures to pass-through the reduction in subsidies to prices by a similar amount (line 4 and calculation 2).

The main cost pressures in 1989 appeared to stem from foreign trade prices. Import prices, in terms of forint, increased by some 15 percentage points more than in 1988. This reflected two factors: (1) the forint/US dollar exchange rate depreciating at a faster rate in 1989 than in 1988; and (2) import prices in US dollar terms rising in 1989, while they fell in 1988. With imports accounting for just over one-third of GDP, this could be expected to raise inflation, as measured by the CPI, by around 5.5 percentage points. Inflation, as measured by the PGDP, would be affected by the rise in import prices only to the extent of the ripple effects on the cost of producing domestic output. An arbitrary estimate of 3.0 percentage points was attributed to this factor (line 5, calculation 3).

As regards export prices in forint terms, they also increased faster in 1989 than in 1988 (by 13.5 percentage points). With exports accounting for a similar share of GDP to imports, this could be expected to raise inflation, as measured by the PGDP, by about 5.5 percentage points. An arbitrary 1 percentage point was added to both the increase in the CPI and the PGDP, to take account of the effect of the increase in the price of exportables consumed domestically.

Increases in interest rates can also generate significant cost pressures when enterprises' outstanding bank loans exceed their deposits. A calculated cost pressure of just over two percentage points is based on the fact that the net outstanding credit position of enterprises with the banking system accounted for just over 30 percent of GDP in 1988 (line 8, calculation 4).

Summing up the various cost pressure components, one derives benchmark estimates for inflation in 1989 of 14.6 percent and 16.9 percent, as measured by the CPI and PGDP, respectively. Such estimates are inevitably crude and should be treated as first approximations to be refined in light of additional information. They do, however, point to a slowing of inflation *based on cost developments*. In fact, inflation in 1989 edged upward, to 17 percent and 18.7 percent, as measured by the CPI and PGDP, respectively. While this discrepancy may, in part, reflect the continuing influence of cost changes in previous periods, it is also likely to be attributable to the *lax financial policies* discussed in Chapter I.

Output

1. The structure of output in Hungary

Industry is the single largest sector in Hungary, accounting for about one third of aggregate value added throughout the 1980s (Table 9). There was some small decline in this share in the second half of the 1980s as industrial output fell on average by 0.2 percent, compared with a positive growth of GDP of 1.6 percent. Nevertheless, industrial output moved generally in step with total GDP (stagnant in 1985–86 and 1988, growing in 1987), until 1989. In that year, the volume of output of nonmaterial services increased by one quarter, while both industrial and agricultural output fell. During the 1980s nonmaterial services were the fastest growing activity and by 1984, at 18 percent of GDP, were firmly established as the second largest sector. Together, all branches of the services sector, defined to include transport and communications, trade, and other material and nonmaterial branches, accounted for over one third of value added, or about the same size as the industrial sector.

Agriculture, the third largest sector, accounted for about 15 percent of total output on average during the 1980s. With favorable weather, agricultural output expanded contracyclically in 1986 and 1988 and decreased (also contracyclically) in 1987 and 1989. Growth in agriculture averaged two tenths of one percent during 1985–89.

2. Determinants of output: demand and supply factors

In a market economy, decisions by enterprises to produce certain goods or services, and by households to consume them, are typically voluntary. The level of public services provided by government will be determined administratively, in response to political processes. For the most part the volume of aggregate output will reflect decisions of individual enterprises. As a general rule, enterprises will increase output when profitability is high or increasing, and conversely.

Macroeconomic analysis does not attempt to track the behavior of individual firms but instead focuses on the overall level of output. The quantity of goods and services that can be produced will vary with the inputs that are used (land, labor, and capital) and the level of available technology, work attitudes, and market structure. 1/ In general, if the quantity of inputs increase or are used more effectively, the *potential output* of the economy expands.

In a market economy, whether firms produce at the maximum potential rate or at less than that rate depends on their actual and prospective sales—i.e., on the

---

1/ Inputs are also referred to as "factors of production" or as "factor services"; workers comprise a factor of production, and the work that is performed is a factor service.

demand for their product. If sales fall below potential output, an individual enterprise will typically adjust downward the volume that it has been producing, possibly laying off some workers. At the macroeconomic level, when demand is weak unemployment in the economy will be higher than normal, and firms will operate at some fraction of their potential level of production. When employees, machines, and buildings are idle, resources are wasted. Potential supply is a kind of upper limit to GDP, but when aggregate demand is less then supply, actual output will initially tend to be limited by demand. 1/

An aggregate production function indicates the relationship between output and the various inputs that constitute factors of production. Formally, the production function may be written as follows:

$$Q = f(K, N, A) \tag{1}$$

Equation (1) states that real output (Q) can change because of increases in the availability of capital (K) and labor (N), and through technological and other improvements (A) that enable existing factor supplies to be used more effectively.

Over time, increases in output must reflect greater availability of factors of production or more efficient factor use. In the short run, growth in real GDP is more likely to reflect changes in the extent to which labor and capital are fully employed. The level of output that would be realized if the labor force were *fully employed*, and labor and capital were used at *normal intensity*, is referred to as *potential* or *full-employment* output. Potential output defined in this way is less than the physical maximum producible with a given capital stock and labor force. The unemployment rate will not be zero at full employment since, in a dynamic economy, some workers are usually between jobs. Similarly, equipment is normally taken out of operation for certain periods of time to allow for maintenance.

While aggregate output may be forced to a level above normal full employment, this is usually associated with increasing costs of production. For example, if laborers work more than the customary number of hours per week, say 40, they would in most cases be paid "overtime," an hourly wage rate 50–100 percent higher than normal for the excess hours. Depreciation of the capital stock would also increase at a higher intensity of production. A firm would normally try to bring its work force into line with its medium-term rate of production so as to avoid these increased costs. However, if demand is very strong in the short run, it may be profitable for a firm to temporarily increase output, the higher costs being passed onto prices.

1/ It should be noted that low *domestic* demand may free goods for export, if exports are determined more by domestic supply than by foreign demand. In this case, the extra foreign spending would substitute for domestic demand and the level of output could be sustained. Also, the presence of unemployed resources, especially in large quantities or if expected to persist, could slow the tendency of prices to creep upward, or even produce a decline in prices, which would generally stimulate demand, output, and employment.

Because the potential level of output refers to use of factors at normal intensity, total output can be higher than potential output, at least for short periods. In general, if aggregate demand is increased, output will tend to be higher, and conversely. Production costs may also be higher, however, especially if the economy is approaching normal full-capacity. Thus, as demand is increased, both some additional output and higher inflation will generally result. The favorable output gains will tend to be large and the inflation effects small if the economy is well below potential output, but price effects will be large and quantity effects small or negligible if output is already at or above the normal full employment level. When aggregate demand is reduced, initially the effects tend to fall primarily on the quantity of output, although in time the inflation rate will also tend to decrease.

For an industrial country with extensive data, the secular growth of potential output may be analyzed with the use of production functions, while short-run determination of output should take into account both *supply* and *demand* factors. Estimates of production functions require adequate data on labor and capital stocks, while formal consideration of the interaction of supply and demand factors depends on a properly articulated econometric model.

Many countries have neither the data nor the models to support such approaches. Consequently, output forecasts in financial programs tend to rely on essentially *ad hoc* procedures. A starting point could be to project output for the forecast year on the basis of *trends* in output growth in the recent period. This could be verified by an analysis of trends in the *sectoral composition* of GDP as, for example, presented in Table 9, but these should be modified to reflect factors specific to each sector and known interrelationships among different activities. For instance, forecasts for agriculture should reflect expectations about weather conditions, producer prices, and other special factors. Forecasts for manufacturing activity could incorporate the reliance of manufacturing on the agricultural sector for inputs. Factors affecting output during periods of *structural change* also need to be considered. Finally, given the role of demand factors in determining output, projections of output need to take account of the stance of *aggregate demand*. In particular, activity in the secondary and tertiary sectors is likely to be sensitive to demand arising from the domestic or external sectors.

Central-Planning and Market Approaches to the Analysis of Aggregate Output

Under central planning, the detailed numerical tables that comprise the plan are simultaneously a means of directing producers, forecasting output, and monitoring the results of government directives. Unemployment and underutilization of productive resources are, in principle, eliminated by keeping demand high relative to supply. The resulting upward pressure on prices is controlled, in turn, by the cost of increased waiting time, or queuing, and by increases in involuntary savings such as in unspendable checking account balances. From the point of view of forecasting it is therefore sufficient to focus on the supply of output in a planned economy. By contrast, aggregate supply and aggregate demand, or spending, need to be considered together in determining output in a market economy.

The elements of an input-output matrix in central-planning describe quantities of output of certain enterprises or branches that are required as inputs by other producers. Additional rows indicate inputs of primary factors (labor, capital, and so forth), and total output; columns show intermediate use, investment, export, and consumption. The division of output between consumption and investment is made administratively and reflects political considerations.

The production function is a major analytical tool in market economies in analyzing the growth of output. Although the voluntary behavior of profit-maximizing enterprises is commonly assumed to underlie the activity represented by a production function, this is not essential; a production function could, in principle, be used to forecast output in a centrally-planned economy, just as input-output analysis is sometimes used in market economies. The production function lacks, however, the details of the operations of individual enterprises or branch industries that is essential to the working of the planning mechanism.

The essential difference between these two approaches is that the production function sacrifices detail but can incorporate the possibility of varying the relative amounts of capital and labor used in the production process. From the point of view of economic theory there are two significant features of this variability that are not allowed for in input-output analysis. One is that the relative economic rewards of labor and capital may change—wages may rise or fall compared to the rate of return on capital. The second is that these relative income changes could induce enterprises to change their mix of factor inputs—to "economize" on labor and use more capital, or vice versa—so that there is a tendency for all available inputs to be fully employed.

Box 1

3. Applications to Hungary

a. Historical trends in output growth

Forecasts of output and prices for Hungary are complicated by the unevenness of developments during the 1980s and the increasing pace of reform toward the end of the decade, GDP growth was close to zero in 1985–86, and again in 1988, but attained favorable rates in 1987 and 1989. (See Tables 9 and 10). The authorities were concerned to limit aggregate demand in order to reduce the deficit on current external transactions in convertible currencies because Hungary had, by the end of the 1970s, already accumulated a large stock of external debt. At the same time, there was a desire to stimulate growth and to increase living standards. The conflict between these two objectives resulted in periods of more expansionary monetary and fiscal policies followed by years of contractionary policies (sometimes called "stop-go" policies). 1/

Fluctuations in domestic demand, however, only partly explain the stagnation-expansion pattern. Aggregate supply was influenced by changes in the share of output allocated to investment, by variation in weather conditions, and by fluctuations in foreign demand for Hungary's exports and changes in their competitiveness. Major reform measures taken in this period may also have affected supply.

While output in the 1980s fluctuated considerably, the trend growth rate was considerably lower than in the previous two decades (Table 3). Notably, aggregate real output in Hungary grew vigorously (by around 6.5 percent) in the decade preceding the first oil-price increase, and at a reduced, but still decent rate (4.9 percent) during the remainder of the 1970s. During the 1980s, however, output growth slowed markedly, averaging 1.6 percent per year in the last five years.

Several hypotheses can be offered in explanation of this medium-term slowdown.

> (1) The level of unemployment remained close to zero during this period, there was no major influx of laborers from neighboring countries, and the population actually declined slightly. Labor-force growth largely reflected increases in participation rates which limited the potential growth of total output.

> (2) The tendency to reduce demand for stabilization purposes by cutting back investment relative to GDP during the 1980s is likely to have had negative effects on growth.

> (3) The higher costs of energy tended to slow the Hungarian economy indirectly as weak demand in the world economy inhibited exports.

1/ For a more detailed account of developments in the 1980s, see Chapter I.

Table 3. Hungary: Growth of Output and Prices by Five-Year Periods

(Annual rates of growth in percent)

	1960/64	1965/69	1970/74	1975/79	1980/84	1985/89
Real NMP	4.4	6.8	6.3	4.6	1.4	0.5
Real GDP			6.3 1/	4.9	1.9	1.6
GDP deflator			1.4 1/	3.7	5.5	10.3
Population			0.3 1/	0.4	-0.1	-0.4

Sources: Row 1 is from Alton's regression averages, reported in Ed A. Hewitt, "The Gross National Product of Hungary," World Bank Staff Working Papers, Number 775 (Washington, D.C.: World Bank, 1985), pp. 16, 19, and from Hungarian sources. Other rows are from IMF, *International Financial Statistics*, except the column for 1985/89, which is from Tables 1 and 2.

1/ Average of rates in 1971-74.

(4) Central planning was able to achieve rapid growth rates in initial years because of the substantial allocation of resources to production of capital goods. Gains from this source, however, eventually decreased, and failed to outweigh the costs of inefficient use of capital and the increasing administrative burden as economies became intrinsically more complex. Moreover, the reform measures introduced were often partial, inconsistent, and subsequently reversed.

(5) Finally, growth rates may eventually decline under central planning because such a system is less attuned to rapid adaptation and full exploitation of the opportunities presented by scientific discoveries and changes in consumers' tastes.

b.   Output during periods of transition

Periods of rapid structural change have often been associated with lower
(higher)—than—expected output growth (losses). It is useful to review at least some
of the *systemic* forces that could be at play in an economy moving from central
planning to market orientation. While by their nature the effects of system factors
are difficult to quantify, they are often the predominant influence over output
developments in periods of transition. Some of the main such factors are listed
below.

(1) The *operating environment* may not be conducive to the complete
abandonment of old for new ways, which may inhibit market generated
supply responses, including investment decisions. For example, the response
to market signals will be weakened if enterprises believe that they will be

85

bailed out of their financial difficulties, either with bank credits and/or budgetary subsidies, and when the initiation of bankruptcy proceedings is not perceived as a real threat.

(2) *Delays in the clarification of property rights* in a system undergoing decentralization may result in upward pressures on wages and a weakened output response to any given change. Take for instance the typical workers of an enterprise who have access to the rents on capital through their influence over the allocation of profits, but do not own the capital. The only channel through which they can share in the benefits of good decision made today that affects future profitability is to remain employed with the enterprise (which death, retirement or dismissal can prevent). Moreover, there is no way in which they can transfer their entitlement to the rents of capital to their heirs.

(3) The change in relative prices induced by liberalization, together with the effects of foreign competition, may render some of the *output unmarketable* at a cost-covering price. Given that it is easier to cut the output of those products that are not in demand than to increase production of those that are, a further transitory cut in output is implied. The need to shift resources from contracting industries to expanding industries as a result of a change in relative prices is similar to the reallocation that would be expected in any economy after, for example, a major devaluation of the exchange rate. In general, the fall in output should be less severe and protracted the smaller are the initial distortions, the more flexibility there is in the system, and the greater is factor mobility.

(4) Movement toward a market mechanism is typically accompanied by strong inflationary pressures as prices, exchange rates and interest rates are liberalized and subsidies are reduced. In order to minimize the disruptions that occur when inflationary pressures begin to create their own inertia, *tight financial policies* are needed. Their contractionary effects tend to initially fall more on output than on prices, reflecting a downward inflexibility of prices. This is particularly so when cost-plus pricing considerations predominate profit incentives.

(5) Price liberalization may also release *monopolistic forces* that had previously been repressed by the mechanisms of central planning and are not as yet effectively checked by competition from alternative domestic or foreign sources of supply. In this case, enterprises would respond by carrying-out a one time increase in prices and reduction in output.

(6) A contraction in *CMEA trade* would be expected to have a significant effect on output, given the noted rigidities in redirecting/transforming the previously exported output to other sectors, e.g., to the convertible currency area. Hungarian officials recently estimated that, other things being equal, a 10 percent decline of exports to the CMEA would result in a decline of GDP of 1 percent.

(7) *Disruptions to, and bottlenecks in,* the distribution networks may initially be in evidence as the existing structures break down and the new ones are not there to replace them.

(8) Finally, *officially reported statistics* may not accurately report actual output developments, at least in the initial stages of reform, because they should largely be based on returns from the existing large socialized enterprises. They may not, therefore, adequately reflect the growing activity of smaller, particularly private, enterprises.

The consequences of the above factors may be exacerbated by the uncertainty of the economic situation and political environment, which may lead many individuals and enterprises to adopt a "wait and see" position—making them reluctant to engage in new activity requiring a longer-term investment in physical or human capital.

Composition of Expenditure

Output can be forecast from both the demand and supply side. By definition, actual expenditure on domestic output will always be equal to the supply of domestic output on an ex-post basis. In a market economy, if the demand for output initially exceeds the supply, some form of adjustment will take place, typically through some combination of higher prices and higher net imports. 1/ A comparison of projections from both the demand and supply sides thus provides a check whether the overall stance of policies, as reflected in demand pressures for domestic output, is consistent with initial supply-side projections for output.

Projections of the composition of expenditure indicate the expected division of domestic demand between consumption and investment as well as the generation of domestic savings. Such forecasts also show the implications of domestic absorption for the external balance.

Forecasts for government consumption and investment should be based on budgetary projections, as discussed in Chapter II. Similarly, the forecasts for exports and imports should be based on balance of payments estimates (Chapter V). Consequently, the sections below concentrate on a projection of household consumption and household and enterprise investment. An overall projection of output from the demand side may need to wait until projections of the monetary, fiscal and external accounts are made.

1. Determinants of household consumption

Household disposable income (YD) can be viewed from the standpoint of either its sources or its uses:

$$YD = W + E + B - T$$
$$= C_H + S_H \qquad (2)$$

where:

W = wages and salaries from the socialized sector and agricultural cooperatives

E = net earning from private activities

B = social benefits

T = taxes less transfers, i.e., direct personal taxes, such as income tax, net of personal transfers, such as pensions and unemployment compensation.

C_H = household consumption

S_H = household savings

1/ By contrast, in a planned economy such an imbalance may manifest itself in shortages, queues, holding of unwanted liquid balances, and proliferation of black markets.

Equation (2) shows that household consumption and household savings are simultaneously determined. For a given level of disposable income, once consumption is known savings is determined as a residual. It also suggests that disposable income is an important determinant of household consumption.

Table 4 summarizes the trends in the relationship between household consumption, on the one hand, and GDP and household disposable income on the other. Between 1980 and 1989 household consumption as a share of GDP was remarkably stable at around 61 percent (column 1). Changes in the share of disposable income consumed (column 2) were broadly offset by changes in the opposite direction in the share of household disposable income in GDP (column 3). For example, in 1985–86 when financial policies were eased and wage gains exceeded increases in profitability, the share of household disposable income in GDP rose substantially at a time when the proportion of income consumed fell. By contrast, in 1989, when profit increases exceeded wage gains, household consumption in relation to disposable income soared dramatically following the liberalization of regulations on personal imports and travel abroad, which released pent-up purchasing power.

As an alternative to extrapolating on the basis of simple ratios, regression techniques may be used to identify behavioral relationships. Specifically, a behavioral relationship between household consumption and household disposable income can be postulated as:

$$C_H = a + bYD \qquad (3)$$

where:

$$a > 0, 0 < b < 1.$$

This specification of the consumption function implies that the marginal propensity to consume (MPC, or $\Delta CP/\Delta YD$) is constant and is equal to b, while the average propensity to consume (CP/YD) falls as YD increases, due to the declining relative importance of a positive constant term. These properties suggest that developments in consumption and savings will help stabilize the economy because the savings ratio tends to rise in booms and decline in slumps. Further, as income grows over time they suggest a long-term rise in the savings ratio.

Other approaches to estimating consumption functions recognize that the consumer is unlikely to be influenced only by income in a particular period. Rather the consumer will consider some longer run or *normal* income stream in determining consumption behavior. For example, during cyclical booms transitory income is positive and the ratio of consumption to *actual* (as opposed to long-run) income would be expected to decline. Similarly, cyclical slumps would be associated with negative transitory income and the ratio of consumption to measured income would be expected to rise. This also suggests that the MPC will be different in the short-run and the long-run. The permanent income hypothesis and the life-cycle theory represent two essentially complementary attempts to make longer-term income concepts operational.

Table 4. Hungary: Household Consumption in Relation to GDP and Disposable Income 1/

	Household Consumption/ GDP (1) = (2)x(3)	Household Consumption/ Disposable Income (2)	Household Disposable Income/ GDP (3)
1975	59.1	92.9	63.6
1976	57.9	93.5	61.9
1977	57.2	92.6	61.8
1978	57.3	92.6	61.9
1979	58.7	94.8	61.9
1980	60.9	95.1	64.0
1981	60.8	94.6	64.3
1982	59.6	93.8	63.6
1983	60.2	92.9	64.9
1984	60.1	92.7	64.8
1985	61.6	91.7	67.2
1986	62.3	90.6	68.8
1987	61.4	91.8	66.9
1988	60.1	92.0	65.3
1989	61.2	99.4	61.6

Source: IMF Institute data base.

1/ In nominal terms.

The permanent income and life-cycle hypotheses of consumption behavior can both be empirically approximated as follows:

$$C_H = B_1 YD + B_2 C_H(-1) \qquad (4)$$

The coefficient B_1 could be interpreted as the short-run MPC to consume and

$\dfrac{B_1}{1 - B_2}$ the long-run MPC.

Table 5 summarizes the results of estimating a consumption function in Hungary using annual data for the period 1975–88. Consumption and income data are defined in real terms. The year 1989 was excluded because, as is evident from Table 4 and was discussed above, the share of disposable income that was consumed in that year was extraordinarily high by historical standards.

Table 5. Hungary: Consumption Functions

Period	Explanatory Variables			
	YD	$C_H(-1)$	Constant	
1975-88	0.83	. . .	70.19	(5)
	(19.16)		(2.35)	
	$R^2 = 0.97$ $\bar{R}^2 = 0.97$		$F_{1,12} = 367.00 > F_{.99} = 9.33$	
1975-88	0.47	0.38	74.15	(6)
	(4.82)	(3.78)	(3.60)	
	$R^2 = 0.99$ $\bar{R}^2 = 0.98$		$F_{2,11} = 393.61 > F_{.99} = 7.20$	

Notes: t-value in parenthesis

C_H = Household consumption in *real* terms, the dependent variable
YD = Household disposable income in *real* terms
$C_H(-1)$ = Household consumption lagged one period.

Equation 5 assumes that the consumption function takes the form of equation (3) of the text. An MPC of 0.83 is estimated. A permanent income approach to Hungarian consumption behavior indicates a short-run MPC of 0.47 and a long-run MPC of 0.76 (Equation 6).

2. Forecasting investment

Gross investment consists of *gross fixed capital formation*, which includes machinery, equipment, and structures, and *changes in inventory* by enterprises. In recent years inventory increases have been equivalent to 0–1.5 percent of GDP annually.

Table 6 summarizes the composition of gross fixed investment by sector. Between 1985 and 1989 *total* fixed investment accounted for 20–25 percent of GDP. *Household investment*, 90 percent of which was in housing, remained relatively small at around 4.5 percent of GDP. The remainder of investment was done by the *public sector*. The distinction between the *government sector* and *public enterprises* was blurred by the fact that the government had the authority to force enterprises to carry out certain investment projects even if they were financed in part or entirely by the enterprises themselves. The classification of fixed capital formation in the accompanying tables is by the entity which paid for the investment, rather than by decision-making authority. The difficulties in attributing separate behavioral relationships to enterprise and government investment decision-making suggests that

Table 6. Hungary: Gross Fixed Investment

(In percent of GDP)

	1985	1986	1987	1988	1989
	(Nominal terms)				
Households	4.4	4.8	4.2	4.3	4.3
Government	6.9	6.5	6.0	6.2	5.8
Enterprises	11.1	12.7	14.6	10.5	10.0
Total	22.4	24.0	24.8	21.0	20.1
	(In constant 1986 prices)				
Households	4.6	4.8	4.3	4.0	4.1
Government	7.4	6.6	6.2	7.0	6.9
Enterprises	11.9	13.0	15.1	12.4	12.9
Total	23.9	24.4	25.6	23.5	23.9

Source: IMF Institute data base.

any discussion of investment should be in terms of the overall public sector. In forecasting a breakdown of investment by entity, however, the government investment figures should coincide with those in the general government accounts.

Among the major factors determining the actual level of investment in Hungary were the official plan; the amount of liquid financial assets held by enterprises; the availability of capital transfers, subsidies, and bank credit; fears of confiscation of assets; and expectations of tax changes. Evaluations based on profitability played a relatively minor role.

While the official plan strongly influenced the rate of real fixed capital formation in the 1970s, the correspondence between plan target and performance became looser during the 1980s (Table 7). This reflected the increased autonomy accorded to enterprises. In addition, the share of enterprise investments financed from their retained earning increased. These developments increased the relative importance of financial policies and discipline in determining the level and composition of investment.

With the exception of 1982, real gross fixed capital formation declined in each year during 1980 to 1985, in part the result of stabilization policies that aimed to reduce domestic demand but protect household consumption levels.

Table 7. Hungary: Annual Percentage Changes in Real Gross Fixed Capital Formation

	Actual	Plan
1971-75	6.9	5.5
1976-80	2.5	2.1
1981-85	-1.6 1/	1.4
1986-90	...	3.5
1979	1.9	...
1980	-5.6	...
1981	-4.3	...
1982	6.4	...
1983	-3.4	...
1984	-3.7	-8.7
1985	-3.0	0.4 to 1.8
1986	2.9	1.5 to 2.0
1987	9.1	1.5 to 2.0
1988	-8.4	-1.0
1989	5.2	6.5
1990	...	3.9

Source: IMF Institute data base.

1/ Simple average.

The 1986–90 five-year plan envisaged a resumption of overall investment growth together with a shift in emphasis toward small- and medium-sized projects to promote structural change and introduce new technologies. Planned increases in real investment were exceeded by modest amounts in 1986 and by over three times the upper target in 1987. During the latter year investment in infrastructure by municipalities recovered, and state enterprises spent heavily in response to buoyant profits, swelled by a boom in consumer spending and easy access to credit and subsidies.

Following the surge of the previous year, a 1 percent reduction in real gross investment was planned for 1988, which proved to be an actual drop of over 8 percent. Large state and municipal projects were curtailed and enterprises' access to state equity loans and credit was tightened. In addition, enterprises delayed investment decisions because of an expected increase, from 20–40 percent, in the rebate from the value added tax on investment expenditures. In the event, public enterprise investment fell by 18 percent in real terms. In 1989 the actual increase in real gross fixed investment of 5.2 percent approximated the plan target of 6.5 percent as credit conditions eased significantly for enterprises as the government adopted an expansionary stance. For 1990, a 3.9 percent increase in real fixed capital formation was planned.

It is interesting to note how the share of output devoted to investment changed relative to the growth of output over the last 10–15 years. An increase in this ratio, commonly referred to as an ICOR (incremental capital output ratio) would indicate that over time the attainment of a given output growth would require increasing amounts of investment. One implication that could be drawn from such a trend is that the efficiency of investment had fallen.

Table 8 calculates ICORs for the 1977–89 period. To minimize the impact of year-to-year fluctuations in this ratio, averages of the last three years were used. ICOR rose from about 6.0 in 1977–79 to a peak of about 21 in 1985–86 before falling back to a range of 10–15 in 1987–89. Developing country ICORs in the mid-1980s ranged from 4 for Asia to 20 for the Middle East and 25 for Africa; hence Hungary was in the middle of the spectrum.

Table 8. Hungary: Calculation of ICOR

	Ratio of real capital formation/real GDP (3 year average) (1)	GDP growth (3 year average) (2)	ICOR (3) = (1)/(2)
1977	32.0	5.8	5.5
1978	32.2	5.2	6.2
1979	31.6	4.8	6.5
1980	30.0	2.4	12.5
1981	28.7	1.9	15.0
1982	27.7	2.0	13.7
1983	26.8	2.6	10.2
1984	26.1	2.5	10.5
1985	24.9	1.3	18.8
1986	24.3	1.0	23.5
1987	24.7	1.6	15.7
1988	24.5	1.6	15.4
1989	24.3	2.4	10.2

Source: Staff estimates.

What factor could be responsible for the deterioration in the productivity of fixed investment in Hungary between the 1970s and 1980s? There was no similar doubling of ICOR in Europe as a whole over this time span. One possibility is that the data do not fully reflect investment and output growth in the expanding private enterprise sector, where fixed capital most likely was more efficient. Another explanation could be that the system of taxing successful enterprises heavily and periodically confiscating their retained profits so as to subsidize loss-making enterprises had increasingly adverse effects on efficiency.

Such practices had at least three different adverse impacts on the level and productivity of fixed investment. First, it was a deterrent to profit-making; hence, generating an operating surplus for financing investment was discouraged. Second, for firms that could generate an operating surplus, the threat of confiscation of financial assets created a strong incentive to transform these financial resources into retained fixed capital as quickly as possible, even if the marginal productivity of additional fixed investment was declining rapidly. Third, making transfers to inefficient enterprises channelled financial resources to either supporting current operations or financing low productivity investments.

Exercises and Issues for Discussion

1. Exercises

For the reference scenario:

a.   Project inflation for 1990, as measured by both the CPI and PGDP, taking account of:

- cost pressures
- the stance of economic policies
- institutional factors
- inflationary expectations

In making these estimates, consideration should be given to the movement in foreign trade prices, provided below:

Total Trade (In Convertible and Nonconvertible Currencies)

	1988	1989	1990
	(percentage change; in U.S. dollar terms)		
Export prices	-0.5	2.6	7.9
Import prices	-3.5	1.4	7.2

b.   Project output from the supply side, using the format of Tables 9 and 10 and taking account of:

- recent trends in output growth and factors particular to the current period
- the stance of economic policies
- the role of structural factors

c.   Project household consumption and total investment in 1990. (An overall projection of output from the demand side, i.e., completion of Tables 11 and 12, and verification that expenditure on domestic output is equal to the supply of domestic output may need to wait until projections 2 of the monetary, fiscal, and external accounts are made.)

2. Issues for discussion

a.   Consider how the projections for output and prices might be affected by the following factors:

- poor weather conditions
- a depreciation of the nominal exchange rate
- an increase in the price of petroleum on world markets
- an easing of monetary and fiscal policies

b.   Discuss possible differences in the behavior of inflation and output in response to the introduction of stabilization programs between economies in transition and market economies. Suggest ways to minimize adverse impacts of stabilization policies on prices and output.

c.   Review the problems of interpreting official measures of prices and output during periods of transition when black markets exist.

Table 9. Hungary: Gross Domestic Product by Sector

(In billions of forint, at approximately 1986 prices) 1/

	1982	1983	1984	1985	1986	1987	1988	1989	1990 Reference Progra
Industry	344.0	350.3	359.2	351.7	350.0	361.8	362.0	355.4	
Agriculture and forestry	172.2	172.3	180.2	173.0	178.9	174.7	188.6	181.8	
Construction	84.6	86.9	82.4	78.0	77.7	82.3	78.3	79.7	
Transport and communications	80.8	81.0	83.4	82.6	85.5	89.8	91.6	96.1	
Trade	100.3	102.6	102.3	105.9	107.4	114.4	101.0	102.0	
Other material branches	20.6	22.4	23.8	25.5	25.9	28.6	27.6	36.8	
Non-material branches	136.7	139.2	145.7	151.7	155.7	168.1	171.2	212.1	
GDP at factor cost	939.1	954.7	976.9	968.4	981.1	1019.7	1020.3	1064.0	
Plus: indirect taxes less subsidies and valuation changes 2/	79.4	85.2	87.8	91.5	91.5	95.1	91.2	86.9	
GDP at market prices	1018.5	1039.9	1064.7	1059.9	1072.6	1114.8	1111.5	1150.9	
Memorandum item: GDP deflator	83.2	86.2	91.9	97.5	101.5	110.0	126.7	150.4	

Source: IMF Institute data base.

1/ The value of the deflator for GDP at market prices in 1986 is 101.5 (see Memorandum item).

2/ Turnover taxes, customs taxes, and other business taxes, less government transfers to enterprises. Also includes valuation changes and a statistical discrepancy.

Table 10. Hungary: Gross Domestic Product by Sector

(In billions of forint, at current prices)

	1982	1983	1984	1985	1986	1987	1988	1989	1990 Reference Program
Industry	290.0	303.8	329.7	351.9	361.0	399.9	430.3	515.3	
Agriculture and forestry	148.5	153.0	166.1	159.4	174.5	189.3	209.3	235.5	
Construction	60.1	65.4	71.1	74.0	79.0	91.6	96.8	114.7	
Transport and communications	70.5	71.4	74.2	77.7	86.3	94.4	101.2	124.2	
Trade	69.9	76.8	86.8	96.7	108.0	128.1	125.9	157.9	
Other material branches	16.2	18.9	21.9	31.3	34.2	30.4	30.6	37.3	
Non-material branches	103.3	112.9	125.4	140.4	154.3	176.7	220.0	308.9	
GDP at factor cost	758.5	802.2	875.2	931.4	997.2	1110.4	1214.1	1493.8	
Plus: indirect taxes less subsidies 1/	89.4	94.2	103.3	102.3	91.6	116.0	194.7	236.6	
GDP at market prices	847.9	896.4	978.5	1033.7	1088.8	1226.4	1408.8	1730.4	
Less: Depreciation	97.3	99.5	105.7	114.3	121.3	127.6	132.6	151.7	
Net domestic product	750.6	796.9	872.8	919.4	967.5	1098.8	1276.2	1578.7	
Memorandum items:									
Net nonmaterial services	54.2	58.8	68.7	77.1	85.6	105.6	131.5	185.3	
Net material product	696.4	738.1	804.1	842.3	881.9	993.2	1144.7	1393.4	

Source: IMF Institute data base.

1/ Turnover taxes, customs taxes, and other business taxes, less government transfers to enterprises. Also includes valuation changes and a statistical discrepancy.

Table 11. Hungary: Components of Aggregate Demand

(In billions of forint at 1986 prices)

	1982	1983	1984	1985	1986	1987	1988	1989	1990 Reference Program
Household consumption 1/	651.4	653.6	660.6	670.6	681.1	700.3	687.2	744.5	
Public consumption	105.5	105.7	107.1	111.4	116.5	117.1	123.5	127.9	
Total consumption	756.9	759.3	767.6	781.9	797.6	817.4	810.7	872.4	
Gross fixed investment	281.5	272.0	261.9	253.8	261.2	284.9	261.2	274.7	
Stockbuilding	-3.1	2.8	6.3	5.3	12.5	-0.5	17.0	0.6	
Gross investment	278.5	274.8	268.1	259.2	273.7	284.4	278.2	275.3	
Domestic demand	1035.4	1034.1	1035.8	1041.1	1071.3	1101.8	1088.9	1147.7	
Exports of goods and nonfactor services 2/	385.7	412.7	441.4	464.7	459.2	486.4	518.5	530.3	
Imports of goods and nonfactor services 2/	402.6	407.0	412.5	445.9	457.9	473.4	495.9	527.1	
GDP at market prices	1018.5	1039.9	1064.7	1059.9	1072.6	1114.8	1111.5	1150.9	
Memorandum item: Distribution of gross fixed investment				253.8	261.2	284.9	261.2	274.7	
Household investment	...	...	...	49.2	51.8	47.4	44.7	46.9	
State investment	...	...	...	78.5	70.4	68.7	78.3	79.8	
Enterprise investment	...	...	...	126.1	139.0	168.8	138.2	148.0	

Source: IMF Institute data base.

1/ Standard definition: consumption of residents at home and abroad.

2/ Standard definition: including foreign tourism.

Table 12. Hungary: Components of Aggregate Demand

(In billions of forint at current prices)

	1982	1983	1984	1985	1986	1987	1988	1989	1990 Reference Program
Household consumption 1/	505.5	540.0	587.6	636.3	678.7	753.3	846.7	1059.8	
Public consumption	84.2	90.9	95.3	104.6	116.0	126.3	157.4	177.7	
Total consumption	589.7	630.9	682.9	740.9	794.7	879.6	1004.1	1237.5	
Gross fixed investment	213.9	220.0	225.4	232.1	261.2	303.5	295.6	348.3	
Stockbuilding	27.9	17.1	26.4	26.3	31.6	24.0	62.6	96.6	
Gross investment	241.8	237.1	251.8	258.4	292.7	327.5	358.2	444.9	
Domestic demand	831.5	868.0	934.7	999.3	1087.4	1207.1	1362.3	1682.4	
Exports of goods and nonfactor services 2/	336.5	378.4	422.9	459.2	459.2	502.3	574.0	678.9	
Imports of goods and nonfactor services 2/	320.2	349.9	379.1	424.8	457.9	483.0	527.5	630.9	
GDP at market prices	847.9	896.4	978.5	1033.7	1088.8	1226.4	1408.8	1730.4	
Memorandum item:									
Distribution of gross fixed investment				232.1	261.2	303.5	295.6	348.3	
Household investment	...	...	...	45.5	51.8	51.5	58.5	73.4	
State investment	...	...	...	71.8	70.4	73.2	88.6	101.2	
Enterprise investment	...	...	...	114.8	139.0	178.8	148.5	173.7	

Source: IMF Institute data base.

1/ Standard definition: consumption of residents at home and abroad.
2/ Standard definition: including foreign tourism.

V. Balance of Payments

Introduction

Listed below are some of the main issues that typically need to be addressed in forecasting a country's balance of payments. Obviously, there are interconnections among these different issues which need to be taken into account in producing a consistent forecast.

(1) External sector forecasts involve interrelationships with the rest of the world and must, therefore, take into account *developments in the world economy*. For example, the values of exports and imports depend on prices of commodities in world markets and the level of economic activity in partner countries. Interest rates in international markets are an important determinant of net interest receipts in the current account and, in relation to domestic interest rates, influence significantly the size and direction of capital flows.

Projections of developments in the world economic environment can be obtained from various private, government, and international institutions. The International Monetary Fund, for instance, publishes a World Economic Outlook twice a year. Nevertheless, a considerable degree of uncertainty must underlie any such forecasts. It is thus useful to undertake sensitivity analyses of the effects of deviations from projected levels of some of the more important external variables, e.g., interest rates, commodity prices, and output growth in industrial countries.

(2) There is considerable diversity in the individual categories of transactions that need to be projected. The types of *behavioral relationships* and *explanatory variables* needed to explain the various items in the trade, services, and capital accounts will, thus, depend on the particular item under consideration. Moreover, there may be deficiencies in the availability and quality of data as well as problems in identifying stable behavioral relationships. The problems may be particularly acute in times of structural change, including changes in the structure of production and commerce such as might result from reforms in the agricultural, financial and trade sectors. Stability of economic relationships may also be affected by changes in policies (for example, trade liberalization by which quantitative restrictions give way to more reliance on the price mechanism) and in economic institutions brought about by changes in political regimes. In such circumstances quantitative forecasts may need to rely heavily on judgement.

(3) In forecasting the balance of payments, *consistency* needs to be achieved with the *other macroeconomic accounts* by taking into consideration factors such as the stance of economic policies, the projected level of economic activity, and the volume of domestic and foreign financial resources required by both the private and public sectors.

(4) A first round of projections for the individual components of the balance of payments may turn out to be inconsistent with the *accounting identity* that external receipts and payments (including reserve movements) must sum to zero, i.e., the sum of current account transactions must equal the sum of capital flows and reserve movements. For example, even though external factors and the stance of domestic policies would seem to suggest a current account deficit, unavailability of capital flows and/or lack of reserves might make this impossible to achieve. Hence, the initial estimates for the current account or the availability of financing would have to be adjusted accordingly.

How the forecast is modified to ensure accounting consistency depends upon the nature of adjustment that is likely to occur. This, in turn is related to the circumstances and the policy orientation of the country. The adjustment process could involve a *depreciation of the currency* and/or the *introduction of other measures* (including use of fiscal and monetary policy) to increase net exports. If, however, the authorities react by intensifying *administrative restrictions* on imports, the adjustment path for exports, domestic output, investment and prices would obviously be different. *External payment arrears* are an extreme form of payments restrictions; this is an unsustainable method of adjustment which will further reduce a country's creditworthiness, and thus its imports, investment, and growth potential.

(5) An important consideration in a forecasting exercise is whether the projected current account outcome is *sustainable*. The ability to attract capital inflows to sustain a current account deficit without running into debt service problems depends, among other things, on the judgment of creditors as to the creditworthiness of the country and how efficiently the borrowed funds are used. In particular, if foreign borrowing is used to finance investments which generate sufficient returns to finance the repayment of such funds, then debt servicing problems should not arise. Debt servicing problems, however, may be expected when resources are used inefficiently or to support domestic consumption only. In addition, changes in world economic conditions may significantly affect the availability and affordability of funds. For example, rising interest rates in the early 1980s exacerbated the debt servicing difficulties experienced by many developing countries.

(6) Finally, the sustainability of any increase or decrease in the current account deficit must be *assessed* in light of developments in the macroeconomic aggregates contributing to those changes. For example, an increase in the current account deficit, rather than reflecting a lack of external adjustment, may stem from a deliberate policy decision to finance a higher level of investment with larger but sustainable capital inflows. Conversely, a reduction in the current account deficit, instead of being due to implementation of an adjustment program, may result from an abrupt reduction in foreign financing, following the absence of an adequate policy response by the authorities to a deteriorating situation.

Forecasting the Balance of Payments

A summary of Hungary's balance of payments in convertible currencies is presented in Table 3 of the statistical appendix. Tables 4–9 of the appendix provide supplementary data required for preparing a balance of payments forecast for 1990. This section briefly reviews determinants of the major items in the balance of payments, and considers special factors that affect their application in Hungary. The workshop emphasizes forecasting transactions with the convertible currency area; data for the nonconvertible balance of payments for 1990 are provided in the relevant appendix tables.

1. Exports

a. Determinants of exports

The value of a country's exports depends on the willingness of foreigners to purchase them, i.e., *the demand for exports*, as well as on the incentives for, and ability of, domestic residents to supply goods for sale abroad, i.e., *the supply of exports*.

Small Country Assumption

A particular market structure relevant to many non–industrialized countries leads to what is referred to as the "small country assumption." On the import side, the small country assumption implies that a nation is sufficiently small in the world market that changes in its demand do not affect the foreign currency price of its imports, i.e., supply is infinitely elastic. For exports, the corresponding assumption is that the country is sufficiently small in the world market that it can sell as much as it likes without affecting the foreign currency price of its exports, i.e., demand is infinitely elastic. As long as these assumptions approximately hold, analysis of trade volumes can focus on demand factors for imports and supply factors for exports. The analysis of foreign currency prices would focus on developments in world markets rather than the actions of the particular country.

Box 1

For countries and commodities where the small country assumption is warranted (see Box 1), the availability of domestic supply acts as the effective constraint on exports. In these cases, an explanation of export volumes requires consideration of the domestic supply process. In principle, the analysis may be broken down into two stages: (1) a review of factors affecting domestic production, and (2) consideration of the proportion of output that is exported. Price incentives play a key role in both stages. The relevant price incentive affecting production is the price of output in domestic currency in relation to the costs of production. The price at which goods can be sold abroad (the world price in domestic currency) relative to the domestic price affects the proportion of supply exported.

Empirical formulations of export supply functions may be based on the following simplified equation:

$$\frac{X}{P_x} = f \left[\underset{(+)}{\frac{P_x}{P_y}}, \ \underset{(+)}{Y_p}, \ \underset{(-)}{DD} \right] \tag{1}$$

where:

$$
\begin{aligned}
X &= \text{value of exports in domestic currency} \\
P_x &= \text{price of exports in domestic currency} \\
P_y &= \text{domestic prices} \\
Y_p &= \text{productive capacity in the export sector} \\
DD &= \text{the volume of domestic demand}
\end{aligned}
$$

The + and − indicate the signs of the partial derivatives of the function, i.e., the expected direction of influence of the independent variables.

The relative price variable reflects the effects of exchange rates, export taxes and subsidies, domestic costs, tariffs and the prices of imported imports. For example, a depreciation of the domestic currency raises the export price received by producers in domestic currency and makes exports more profitable relative to selling domestically. A subsidy given to exports has a similar incentive effect and an export tax lowers the actual price received by the exporter. Import tariffs and other factors adding to the costs of production reduce the relative price of exports. The existence of a given productive capacity in the export sector sets limits on the amount of exports. In practice, it is often difficult to obtain empirical estimates for this variable. If exportable products are also sold in the domestic market, the level of aggregate demand in the home country is likely to affect exports. With a given productive capacity in the export sector, a fall in domestic demand will induce producers to expand their sales abroad in order to maintain profitability.

The situation is more complicated when a country is sufficiently important in world markets that its actions can affect the world price. The prices and volumes in world markets are then determined by the interaction of demand and supply, and therefore both need to be assessed to obtain a projection of the value of exports. In general, the demand for exports depends on the level of income and expenditures in the trading partner countries, as well as the price of exports relative to that of goods produced domestically in these countries.

A demand function for exports could be specified as follows:

$$\frac{X}{P_x} = f\left[\frac{WD}{P_w}, \frac{P_x}{P_n}\right] \qquad (2)$$

$$(+) \ (-)$$

where:

X = value of exports in domestic currency
WD = world demand in domestic currency
P_x = price of exports in domestic currency
P_w = world prices in domestic currency
P_n = price of trading partners import substitutes in domestic currency

This equation shows the demand for exports as a function of world demand for a country's products and its competitiveness. Construction of appropriate scale and relative price variables requires information on trading partner countries' incomes and prices, averaged using appropriate weights.

In principle, simultaneous consideration of supply and demand factors requires a more complex econometric specification. To some extent forecasting may be simplified by disaggregation into products where supply- or demand-side considerations predominate.

b. Special factors affecting exports in Hungary

Convertible currency exports were *liberalized* continuously in the 1980s. In particular, the state monopoly of foreign trade was removed, the number of enterprises allowed to export and import expanded, and the number of items on the negative list reduced. The authorities tried to ensure the competitiveness of Hungarian exports by depreciating the forint a number of times, most recently in December 1989 (Table 5). Other incentives used to stimulate convertible currency exports included rebates of the differential producers' turnover tax that was in effect from 1980 to 1988, subsidies for exports with agricultural and food processing content, the so-called modernization grants, incentives for export-related investment based on preferential credits and interest rates, as well as various other forms of tax rebates.

In the period under review the *CMEA* had an important impact on Hungary's foreign trade. Under these arrangements, essential imports of energy and raw materials were paid for by exports of Hungarian agricultural and industrial products. The ruble area exports were influenced by governmental protocols and to some extent domestic liquidity concerns, rather than by the market related considerations affecting convertible currency exports. Exports to the ruble area were in general characterized by standards of quality, packaging, delivery and servicing of products that were less stringent than in the convertible currency

109

markets (or even domestically). The incentives offered to exporters to the ruble area were also different from those affecting convertible currency area exports. As the trade was conducted under government agreements, the enterprises received immediate payment in forint upon delivery of goods. At times, ruble exports were used by enterprises to shore up their liquidity positions. Further, enterprises received compensation from the budget for differences in profitability between exporting to the nonconvertible area and selling in convertible currencies or to the domestic market. The amount of compensation allowed was reduced in 1988–89.

As previously mentioned, this workshop concentrates on the techniques required to forecast the convertible currency balance of payments, with limited attention given to transactions with the ruble area. However, allowance needs to be made for possible connections between convertible and ruble transactions. For example, an inability to export to the ruble area might add pressure on enterprises to increase sales in convertible currencies, or vice versa.

The limited time series on trade data available for Hungary, as well as the substantial structural and other changes affecting the economy, restrict the use of regression analysis for forecasting exports. Consequently, reliance has to be placed on more judgmental methods. For this purpose, Table 1 provides data on export volumes and empirical approximations of some of its main determinants as reviewed above.

Indicators are presented of export competitiveness and profitability and the growth of export markets. In the Hungarian system it is possible that a tight liquidity constraint may compel enterprises to intensify their efforts to export. Financial constraints are proxied by enterprise deposits with the banking system and bank credit to enterprises. Data are also presented on the volume of ruble exports to facilitate consideration of possible substitution between ruble and convertible currency exports.

Table 1. Hungary: Nonruble Exports and Selected Indicators

(Percentage changes)

	1983	1984	1985	1986	1987	1988	1989
Value of nonruble exports 1/	0.3	− 1.8	− 8.5	0.1	11.6	16.5	3.4
Volume of nonruble exports	6.4	0.4	-6.6	-3.9	5.0	8.8	2.7
Export prices in U.S. dollars	− 5.7	-6.2	-2.0	4.1	6.3	7.1	0.7
Export prices in SDRs	-3.7	-2.2	-1.0	-8.9	-3.3	3.1	5.7
Exchange rate (SDR/forint, period average) 2/	-11.3	-7.4	-3.2	-5.4	-11.5	-10.4	-10.5
Domestic currency price of exports 3/	7.6	5.2	2.2	3.5	8.2	13.5	16.2
GDP deflator	3.6	6.6	5.8	4.5	8.5	15.1	18.2
Domestic demand deflator	4.5	7.5	6.4	5.7	7.9	14.2	17.1
Real effective exchange rate	-4.6	1.5	3.3	-10.3	-10.0	2.9	0.8
Growth in export markets	--	--	--	3.3	3.4	4.2	3.3
Enterprise deposits with banks	-11.3	-7.0	16.5	-1.5	17.7	-12.7	26.0
Bank credit to enterprises	2.7	5.7	9.1	12.1	6.2	-1.8	21.3
Volume of ruble exports	--	--	8.3	-0.1	2.5	0.6	-13.5

Source: IMF Institute data base.

1/ U.S. dollar value of exports.
2/ A negative number implies a depreciation of the forint in relation to SDR.
3/ Approximated as the percentage change in the SDR price plus percentage change in the SDR/forint exchange rate.

2. Imports

a. Determinants of imports

Application of the small country assumption allows the volume of imports to be forecast on the basis of demand factors. Import prices (in foreign currency) would then need to be determined from an analysis of world markets and developments in particular trading partner countries. An import demand equation could be specified as follows:

$$\frac{IM}{P_m} = f \left[\frac{Y_d}{P_y}, \; \frac{P_m}{P_y} \right] \tag{3}$$
$$\quad\quad\;\; (+) \;\; (-)$$

where:

IM = value of imports
P_m = domestic currency price of imports
Y_d = domestic income (or domestic demand)
P_y = domestic prices (GDP or domestic demand deflator)

Import volumes in this equation are related to scale and relative price variables. Usually, the scale variable is either real income or domestic expenditure. Imports would be positively related to either variable. The price competitiveness variable shows the response of imports to changes in relative prices. A negative relationship is indicated showing that as the relative price of imported goods rises, there is a tendency to reallocate expenditure towards domestic goods. The domestic purchaser, in considering whether to buy domestic or imported goods, would compare the relative prices in the same currency. Consequently, changes in the relative price variable can reflect both movements of domestic and foreign prices in their respective currencies and alterations in the exchange rate. Changes in the rate of import duty have a similar impact on the relative prices as the exchange rate.

The appropriate specification of an import demand equation varies for different types of goods. Therefore, disaggregating imports into subcategories such as capital, intermediate and consumption goods, and relating them to different scale and relative price variables can improve the reliability of estimated behavioral relationships. For example, it may be expected that capital goods imports are dependent on investment activity and imports of consumer goods on consumption. Moreover, the price indices of domestically produced competing goods can move quite differently for various categories of imports.

Several other factors, apart from income and relative price effects may influence the level of imports. Particularly important, among such factors, may be the availability of credit. This variable may affect imports indirectly through its impact on the growth of domestic demand components. A more direct effect occurs where it acts as the effective constraint on imports. Imports in many countries are influenced by various forms of quantitative restrictions as well as by tariffs and other measures which affect the price of such goods. Allowance needs to be made for the effects of any changes in these restrictions on the level of imports. In countries where imports are substantially rationed, the availability of foreign exchange may be an important factor influencing legal changes in restrictions or their effective implementation.

b. Special factors affecting imports in Hungary

All imports were subject to general quantitative restrictions until 1984, when quotas on imports of capital goods and productive inputs were removed. Instead, these were placed under a licensing scheme, which provided for a semi-automatic right for license holders to bring in goods outside a so called negative list. In contrast, imports of consumer goods remained subject to a quota. The set of enterprises able to obtain import licenses was also expanded in stages between 1986 and 1988, at which point practically all enterprises became eligible to trade in goods outside the negative list. A further liberalization took place at the beginning of 1989, when licensing restrictions were abolished for goods representing 40 percent of 1988 imports, and the universal quota on consumer goods imports was relaxed significantly. Tariffs on non-ruble imports were also gradually lowered in the 1980s, according to Hungary's commitments under the GATT.

Table 2 provides data on import values and volumes, and empirical approximations of some of the main determinants of the latter. Import values show large increases in 1986–87. However, to a substantial extent these increases reflected a depreciation of the dollar against other major currencies. To better reflect the foreign currency prices of average imports, the table shows import prices in SDRs as well as in U.S. dollars.

Data are included on a number of variables that might be used to explain the behavior of imports. Changes in real GDP and domestic demand represent scale effects. Competitiveness can be assessed by comparing fluctuations in the domestic currency prices of imports and the GDP deflator. In addition, the table includes changes in the volume of ruble imports to help assess whether any obvious substitution has taken place between the two types of imports.

In a situation where quantitative estimation of behavioral relationships is difficult, a useful starting point may be to compare estimates with those observed in other countries. Also, if estimates are available for a wide variety of countries and product groups, these may establish a likely range of acceptable results. Box 2 presents a summary of some available results for price and income elasticities of trade flows.

Table 2. Hungary: Nonruble Imports and Selected Indicators

(Percentage changes, unless otherwise indicated)

	1983	1984	1985	1986	1987	1988	1989
Value of nonruble imports 1/	−1.3	−3.5	1.3	13.4	9.1	−1.4	3.1
Volume of nonruble imports	6.4	0.4	2.6	0.7	2.5	−6.9	4.9
Import prices in U.S. dollars	−7.2	−3.8	−1.3	12.6	6.4	5.9	−1.7
Import prices in SDRs	−4.2	0.2	−0.3	0.4	−2.6	1.9	4.3
Domestic currency price of imports 2/	7.1	7.6	2.9	5.8	8.9	12.3	14.8
GDP deflator	3.6	6.6	5.8	4.5	8.5	15.1	18.2
Relative price change 3/	3.5	1.0	−2.9	−1.3	0.4	−2.8	−3.4
Real GDP	2.1	2.4	−0.4	1.2	3.9	0.3	3.5
Real domestic demand	−0.1	0.2	0.5	2.9	2.8	−1.2	5.4
Volume of Ruble imports	--	--	−0.4	3.8	3.7	4.0	−17.1
Nonruble imports in percent of GDP	21.2	21.1	21.1	20.8	20.6	19.0	18.7

Source: IMF Institute data base.

1/ In U.S. dollars.
2/ Approximated as the percentage change in the SDR price plus percentage change in the exchange rate.
3/ The difference in the percentage changes in the domestic currency price of imports and the GDP deflator.

3. Services and transfers

a. Determinants of services and transfers

Services form a rather heterogenous group of transactions. The following indicates some of the determinants of major categories.

> (1) **Freight and insurance** receipts and payments are related to the movements of exports and imports, respectively. In practice, payments may be estimated in the official statistics on the basis of a fixed ratio of f.o.b. import values.

(2) **Other transportation**, i.e., port and passenger services, are also influenced by merchandise trade flows, as well as factors that affect the overall level of tourism and the competitive situation of domestic carriers.

(3) **Travel** receipts and payments may be affected by income and price competitiveness variables. Receipts may be influenced by incomes in the countries from which travelers come as well as by the cyclical situation in those countries. Analysis of price competitiveness effects may be complex, involving a comparison of movement of prices and exchange rates between exporting and importing nations as well as with other competing countries. International transportation costs can also be an important factor influencing tourism flows. In the short run tourism may be substantially disrupted by social and political instability. Improvements in tourist services, for example hotels, may have important effects on travel flows over a longer period.

(4) **Investment income** arising from direct and other investment may be differentiated. The former depends on past accumulated foreign investment and may take place only after significant time has elapsed due to legal restrictions on the repatriation of funds. For other investment income, interest payments and receipts reflect the amount and cost of past and current foreign borrowing and lending, as well as the level of international reserves.

(5) **Workers' remittances** often form the major component of private unrequited transfers. A distinction may be drawn between the total earnings of workers in the host country and the amount which is repatriated. Total earnings may vary according to the cyclical situation in the host country. Repatriation of earnings are influenced by incentives to return funds, including exchange rate expectations and tax factors. Balance of payments forecasts of *official unrequited transfers* should be consistent with budgetary estimates of foreign grants.

b.   Factors affecting services in Hungary

An analysis of Hungary's balance of payments, especially in convertible currencies (Table 3), shows that service transactions have played a particularly important role in the late 1980s. Service transactions were the main factor behind movements in the current account in 1988-89, mainly due to the unprecedented expansion in travel spending (including purchases abroad of consumer durables). This was a direct result of policy changes by the authorities. Beginning in 1988, Hungarian travel regulations underwent a significant liberalization: passport regulations were relaxed, so that issued passports became valid for travel in all countries within a five year period; access of residents to foreign exchange for travel purposes was greatly expanded; customs regulations for private imports were relaxed by expanding the duty free allowance and lowering the customs duties on private imports of personal cars; and holdings of foreign currency accounts were made easier as residents were allowed to declare convertible currency holdings from non-specified sources.

In forecasting the service account for Hungary in 1990, the following factors may be considered:

(1) **Freight and insurance**. Available data show only net flows, making it more difficult to detect empirical regularities between freight and trade transactions. Freight and insurance (net) may be compared with exports, imports and the trade balance; the most promising relationship appears to be between imports and net freight payments.

(2) **Travel**. Measured in U.S. dollars, receipts from tourism increased steadily if not spectacularly until 1985, and accelerated in 1986 and afterwards. These data are, however, affected by the appreciation of the dollar up to 1985 and its subsequent depreciation. If data were presented in SDRs, the rise would have been more pronounced up to 1985 and less so in 1986-87. The rather dramatic movements in travel debits in 1988-89 can be related to the institutional changes described above.

(3) **Investment income**. Issues related to interest payments are discussed in the section on debt and medium term balance of payments projection. Investment income credits relate largely to the level of reserves and international interest rates, as Hungary has few other foreign assets. In any event, this item is relatively small and does not show much variation.

(4) **Other services** (net) have also been relatively small and have not been subject to wide movements. Simple time trends may be used to get an acceptable projection for 1990.

In the case of Hungary, *unrequited transfers* have originated almost exclusively from private sector transactions, which have shown a steadily rising trend over the years.

4. Capital transactions

a. Determinants of capital flows

Capital movements can be divided into three main categories: direct investment, medium and long-term capital and short-term flows. Further disaggregation can be made within these categories, for example, between official and private capital, as well as between portfolio investment and project loans and trade related credits. Such disaggregation is useful for the purposes of forecasting, as the economic agents involved in the various transactions can be expected to behave quite differently.

The amount of direct investment is related to the presence of investment opportunities and the prospects of rapid economic growth. Clear rules and regulations are part of a favorable investment climate, as are credible government policies designed to achieve macroeconomic stability.

Projections of inflows of official medium- and long-term capital can use information from the budget and development plans, as well as from the donors. Private flows are by their nature more difficult to forecast. For many countries, access to international bank lending is limited and tends to vary with conditions prevailing in the international capital markets. Creditworthiness can be influenced by general prospects of the balance of payments, including the stance of economic policies.

In cases where capital flows respond to market forces—i.e., where there are few restrictions to capital flows and there is some substitutability between domestic and foreign securities—interest rate differentials play an important role, with funds tending to move from lower to higher interest rate markets. The effect of interest rate differentials need, however, to be viewed in the context of expectations about the exchange rate. More generally, the political and social situation is likely to be an important factor affecting the assessment of the risk involved in long-term capital flows. Provision of trade credit may be related to trade flows. In addition, the extent of reliance on external trade credits may be affected by monetary policy and the availability of domestic credit. Short-term capital flows can at times react very quickly to variations in financial market conditions between countries.

b. Factors affecting the capital account of Hungary

Hungary was an active participant in the international capital markets in the second half of the 1980s. Convertible currency capital account transactions shifted from a net outflow in 1982 to a net inflow of $1.5 billion in 1985. The inflows came largely in the form of long and medium-term capital, with short-term capital flows fluctuating considerably over the period. Hungary enjoyed a relatively high credit rating from 1984 to 1989; in addition to receiving international bank loans, it was able to place notes and bonds in world financial markets.

Issues closely related to capital transactions are further discussed in the section on external debt below.

Forecasting External Debt

This section reviews the determinants and assessment of external debt, developments in the external debt of Hungary, and a methodology for medium-term balance of payments and debt projections. Supporting data on Hungary's external debt are presented in Statistical Appendix Tables 11–13.

1. Determinants and assessment of external debt

a. Definition and linkages

Gross external debt may be defined as "the amount, at any given time, of disbursed and outstanding contractual liabilities of residents of a country to nonresidents to repay principal, with or without interest, or to pay interest, with or without principal."[1] Forecasting and assessment of external debt requires consideration of the linkages with the balance of payments and other macroeconomic data.

Linkages between the balance of payments and external debt are reflected in the following equation:

Increases in gross external debt (4)

    = current account deficit
    − non-debt creating (equity) capital inflows
    + official reserve increase
    + acquisition of assets abroad by the private sector

Equation (4) shows that an increase in gross external debt can have three broad sources: current account deficits not financed by non-debt creating inflows, borrowing to finance an official reserve build-up, and private capital flight. It also summarizes the factors that need to be forecast, or assumed, to allow projections of external debt.

Linkage with the current account emphasizes the relationship between external debt and other macroeconomic developments. Thus, to the extent that external debt is financing a current account deficit this implies that a country's domestic expenditure is in excess of its income. Alternatively, this may be viewed as an excess of investment over domestic savings. [2]

---

[1] *External Debt: Definition, Statistical Coverage and Methodology*, a report by an international working group on external debt statistics of the World Bank, IMF, BIS and OECD.

[2] See Workshop on Interrelations Among Macroeconomic Accounts (Chapter II).

b. Assessment of external debt

By increasing the total amount of resources available, external debt can contribute to a country's long-run growth potential and welfare. Borrowed resources may also smooth the impact of temporary shocks that reduce consumption and investment. However, debt policies cannot be viewed as independent of other macroeconomic policies. External borrowing needs to be consistent with both short-term *macroeconomic objectives* and *medium-term balance of payments viability*. The following points should be emphasized in this context.

(1)   Total financial flows—from both domestic and external sources—should support a level of aggregate demand that is compatible with domestic and external balance. From this point of view, one of the purposes of external debt management is to complement policies influencing such variables as domestic credit expansion to ensure that aggregate demand is maintained within appropriate bounds. For example, in the case of a domestic imbalance arising from too large a public sector deficit, control of public sector external borrowing directly complements limitations on public sector domestic financing.

(2)   Current borrowing implies future payments of *interest* on the stock of outstanding debt, which can be approximated by the appropriate interest rate (e.g., LIBOR or prime rate plus a spread) multiplied by the average stock of debt over a given period and *principal* (typically there is a fixed repayment schedule of the existing debt stock, e.g., a repayment period of 10 years with 6 years grace period could imply four equal annual installments starting in the seventh year). Together, these payments constitute *debt-service* obligations due.

(3)   Unless these debt-servicing costs can be financed in the medium-term, a country will face external payments difficulties; as a result it may have to undertake more policy and expenditure adjustments than if a less ambitious debt policy had been pursued, reducing and/or eliminating the gains already achieved in terms of economic growth and welfare.

(4)   Debt management may be complicated by uncertainties relating to many of the main determinants of debt capacity, e.g., the growth of exports, the terms of new debt, and international interest rates.

Several factors may contribute to achieving a *sustainable external debt position*.

(1)   The borrowed funds must be used productively so that the economy's potential to generate foreign exchange is increased.

(2)   Sound macroeconomic policies must be followed. For example, the maintenance of an overvalued exchange rate has often been associated with the financing of capital flight: the central bank borrows abroad and sells

foreign exchange to private residents, who use the proceeds to acquire foreign assets.

(3)   An ability to obtain external resources needed to service the debt. Creditors' willingness to increase their exposure in a country is strongly linked to how their perceptions of points (1) and (2) above.

(4)   A favorable external environment.

c.   Debt indicators

Some commonly used indicators of a country's external debt position are presented in Box 3. While useful, such indicators are inevitably partial. An assessment of the sustainability of a country's external debt position needs to be based on a broader view of the appropriateness of the macroeconomic policy stance and the external prospects. Consideration also needs to be given to the structure of debt and, in some cases, possibilities for debt restructuring.

Debt Indicators

Debt ratios offer various measures of the cost of, or capacity for, servicing debt in terms of the foreign exchange or output forgone. Exports of goods and services and gross national product may be used as scaling factors. Both stock and flow indicators are used in assessing a country's external debt situation. The former emphasize the extent of past dependence on contractual capital inflows. Flow indicators are often used as indices of short-run rigidity in a country's balance of payments; the higher the ratio, the greater the external adjustment required to compensate for adverse balance of payments developments. The following are frequently referred to measures:

   •   debt outstanding and disbursed to exports of goods and services;

   •   debt outstanding and disbursed to gross national product;

   •   total debt service to exports of goods and services (the debt-service ratio); and

   •   total debt service to gross national product.

Although these ratios may be helpful in signaling possible debt problems, two countries facing similar ratios may face considerably different economic circumstances. A full assessment of a country's debt position requires consideration of the overall macroeconomic situation and balance of payments prospects.

Box 3

121

2. Hungary: External debt background and current prospects

Partly because of a delayed response to sharp increases in world prices for oil and other imported raw materials, Hungary's convertible currency trade deficit widened steadily in the 1970s, resulting in a substantial build-up of external debt. External indebtedness declined during the period 1980–82, but subsequently rose from US$10.2 billion in 1982 to about US$20 billion at end-December 1987 (Table 11). Most of this increase reflected unfavorable developments in the current account of the balance of payments as well as periodic outflows of short-term capital. There was, however, also a valuation effect from the depreciation of the U.S. dollar against other major currencies, as a substantial part of Hungary's debt is denominated in deutsche marks and Japanese yen.

In 1988 the convertible current account deficit narrowed and capital outflows ceased: as a result external debt virtually remained at the 1987 level. However, in 1989 looser financial policies and larger debt service payments led to a widening of the current account deficit, and outstanding external debt in convertible currencies increased by US$1 billion. The debt structure, on the other hand, improved markedly during the second half of the 1980s because of successful refinancing operations. Short-term debt, declined from one-third of total debt in 1983, to only 16 percent in 1989.

Total debt service payments increased rapidly during the period 1982–86 because of the relatively short maturity span of loans contracted in the early 1980s as well as the prepayment of certain future maturities. From 1986 to 1989, however, debt service payments declined from 87 to 48 percent of exports of goods and services, reflecting several refinancing operations (Table 12).

Medium-term prospects are largely dependent upon the balance of payments performance and developments in international interest and exchange rates, as well as lenders and investors' continuing willingness to provide additional resources. A greatly expanded recourse to bond markets in recent years made it possible for Hungary to withstand a reduction of commercial bank exposure. However, access to external capital was threatened by the poor performance of 1989. Meanwhile, rolling over the principal on debt incurred prior to 1990 alone will require gross annual borrowing of between US$2.0 and US$ 2.5 billion (Table 13).

3. Medium term balance of payments projections

Medium-term projections are required to assess the viability of the balance of payments and the sustainability of the external debt position. Use of Lotus worksheets can greatly facilitate the preparation of such projections. A simple worksheet has been prepared for this purpose which can be used to calculate the debt and debt service implications of possible medium-term balance of payments developments. 1/ Specifically, starting from the balance of payments and external debt projections already derived for 1990, a targeted level of international reserves is determined for 1991–94 and, given projected current account developments in these years, the capital account is obtained residually.

A key feature of the worksheet is that it explicitly allows for the linkages between balance of payments developments and the external debt position. Thus, for example, an increase in the external debt would reflect the financing needs generated from the successive current account deficits; similarly investment income debits, i.e., interest payments, in the current account would be affected by changes in the stock and the terms of the external debt.

The worksheet consists of four parts. Section I summarizes the assumptions that need to be inputted into the worksheet to generate balance of payments projections for 1991–94, using 1990 as the base year. These include:

(1) rates of growth for all the components of the external current account balance—with the exception of interest payments—as well as for short-term capital flows and net direct investment;

(2) A targeted level of gross official international reserves;

(3) interest rates to be applied to the external debt; and

(4) rates of growth for real GDP and partner country GDP deflator denominated in U.S. dollars. Assuming domestic prices in U.S. dollar terms increase at the same rate as those of partner countries, a value of nominal GDP in U.S. dollar terms can be estimated and used as a scale variable to measure the relative size of the projected external current account imbalances and debt and debt service burdens. 2/

Section II summarizes the medium-term balance of payments projections that stem from the assumptions inputted in Section I. Medium- and long-term disbursements and interest payments on medium- and long-term debt are determined endogenously and simultaneously. The former is determined residually by the financing needs of the external current account balance, taking into account short-term capital flows and net direct investment, whereas the latter is based on the average outstanding stock of debt and the relevant interest rate. Interest payments on short-term debt also are determined endogenously.

Section III summarizes selected external indicators that result from the balance of payments projections. They are relevant in assessing the viability and sustainability of the scenario.

1/ A diskette for the workshop is available.
2/ This implicitly assumes that the real effective exchange rate remains unchanged at its 1990 level.

Section IV summarizes the working tables that were used to calculate interest obligations on the external debt. As inputs for this calculation, a repayment schedule for debt incurred prior to 1990 is used based on Table 13; for debt incurred since 1990, a repayment period of eight years with a two year grace period was assumed. LIBOR was used as the relevant interest rate to be applied to the outstanding debt stock. It should be noted, however, that in recent years the average interest rate paid by Hungary has been somewhat below the LIBOR rates on one year deposits. This may reflect the large proportion of Hungary's debt to official creditors at concessional rates, and the currency composition of the debt.

An example of the use of the worksheet is presented in Table 14. For illustrative purposes, hypothetical figures were inserted for 1990 and the following assumptions were made for the 1991-94 period.

(1) **Current account.** Annual growth rates in the values of exports and imports of 10 percent and 8 percent, respectively. A 5 percent annual growth rate in the net position for other services; investment credits and transfers are calculated using annual growth rates of 10 percent. LIBOR is used as the relevant interest rate.

(2) **Reserve target.** This is set at the equivalent of about 3.5 months of imports.

(3) **Capital account.** Net inflows of short-term capital and direct investment each rise by 10 percent annually.

Exercises and Issues for Discussion

1. Exercises

a.   Prepare a forecast of the balance of payments for Hungary in convertible currencies for 1990 using the format of Statistical Appendix Table 3. The forecast should use the methodology and information provided in this workshop and the forecasts for world market and other exogenous factors presented in Table 5. The projections should be consistent with those developed in other workshops and in particular that on Prices, Output, and Expenditure.

b.   Develop a medium-term projection of Hungary's balance of payments and external debt situation for the period 1990–94. These projections should use the worksheet and methodology presented in this workshop. Reference should be made to the WEO projections for 1990–94 in Table 5.

2. Issues for discussion

a.   Review the acceptability of the balance of payments projection prepared for 1990. To the extent that the forecast indicates problems in 1990 (for example, the financing requirements is unrealistically high, pointing to the emergence of a financing gap) what are the major options open to the authorities?

b.   Consider any special factors that may affect balance of payments projections for economies in transition from centrally-planned to market economies.

c.   Comment on the possible impact of changes in the following items on the forecasts for the current and capital accounts:

- Domestic credit
- Domestic absorption
- The exchange rate
- Foreign or domestic interest rates

d.   On the basis of results of exercise 1.b, assess the medium-term viability of the balance of payments and the sustainability of the external debt position. To the extent that you detect problems review the policy options available to the authorities.

e.   Consider the major uncertainties in the medium-term projections and their possible effects on the outcome. Review the possible impact of different assumptions for key variables (e.g., foreign trade prices, international interest rates, etc.) on the medium-term projections. Further simulations of the model used in exercise 1.b may facilitate this analysis.

f.   Review modifications that might be incorporated into the spreadsheet to allow for a fuller analysis of medium-term developments and the impact of policy measures.

Table 3. Hungary: Balance of Payments in Convertible Currencies

(In millions of U.S. dollars)

	1982	1983	1984	1985	1986	1987	1988	1989	1990 Reference	1990 Program
Trade balance	668.0	773.0	891.0	128.0	-482.0	37.0	489.0	536.0		
Exports	4831.0	4832.0	4916.0	4188.0	4186.0	5051.0	5505.0	6446.0		
Imports	-4163.0	-4059.0	-4025.0	-4060.0	-4668.0	-5014.0	-5016.0	-5910.0		
Services (net)	-1028.0	-755.0	-889.0	-1035.0	-1087.0	-1018.0	-1408.0	-2100.0		
Freight and insurance, net	-222.0	-164.0	-154.0	-156.0	-237.0	-309.0	-299.0	-310.0		
Travel (net)	180.0	167.0	165.0	147.0	199.0	367.0	41.0	-349.0		
Credits	264.0	256.0	268.0	281.0	364.0	553.0	670.0	738.0		
Debits	-84.0	-89.0	-103.0	-134.0	-165.0	-186.0	-629.0	-1087.0		
Investment income (net)	-1118.0	-758.0	-816.0	-833.0	-963.0	-988.0	-1076.0	-1386.0		
Credits	79.0	97.0	128.0	186.0	252.0	235.0	230.0	219.0		
Debits	-1197.0	-855.0	-944.0	-1019.0	-1215.0	-1223.0	-1306.0	-1605.0		
Other current payments (net)	132.0	0.0	-84.0	-193.0	-86.0	-88.0	-74.0	-55.0		
Unrequited transfers (net)	61.0	53.0	63.0	61.0	74.0	102.0	115.0	126.0		
Current account	-299.0	71.0	65.0	-846.0	-1495.0	-879.0	-804.0	-1438.0		
Medium- and long-term capital	-43.4	-158.4	1298.5	1692.7	1107.1	1109.8	690.5	1563.1		
Assets (net)	-510.0	-185.0	-43.0	-240.0	-79.0	-84.0	-26.0	32.0		
Liabilities (net)	466.6	26.6	1341.5	1932.7	1186.1	1193.8	716.5	1351.1		
Disbursements	1701.6	1522.6	3102.5	4513.0	4105.0	3364.0	2565.5	3091.2		
Amortizations	-1235.0	-1496.0	-1761.0	-2580.3	-2918.9	-2170.2	-1849.0	-1740.1		
Direct capital investment								180.0		
Short-term capital	-708.0	438.0	-1247.2	-170.0	79.3	-770.8	65.0	-218.0		
(including errors and omissions)										
Total Capital account	-751.4	208.6	51.3	1522.7	1186.4	339.0	755.5	1345.1		
Overall balance	-1050.4	279.6	13.7	676.7	-308.6	-540.0	-48.5	-92.9		
Financing	1050.4	-279.6	-13.7	-676.7	308.6	540.0	48.5	92.9		
Change in reserves (inc=-)	813.0	-635.0	-449.2	-766.4	-260.5	893.8	182.0	251.0		
Use of Fund credit	237.4	355.4	435.5	-89.7	-48.1	-353.8	-133.5	-158.1		
Purchases	237.4	355.4	435.5	0.0	0.0	0.0	221.5	65.8		
Repurchases	0.0	0.0	0.0	-89.7	-48.1	-353.8	-355.0	-223.9		

Source: IMF Institute data base.

Table 4. Hungary: Nonruble Trade, Customs Basis

(In millions of US$ and percentage change)

	1982	1983	1984	1985	1986	1987	1988	1989	1990 Reference	Program
Exports, fob	4974.3	4989.2	4899.4	4483.3	4485.7	5005.7	5833.0	6030.0		
(percent change)		0.3	-1.8	-8.5	0.1	11.6	16.5	3.4		
Exports fob, 1986 prices	4487.1	4774.3	4998.3	4667.1	4485.7	4709.0	5123.5	5259.8		
(percent change)		6.4	0.4	-6.6	-3.9	5.0	8.8	2.7		
Export prices, 1986=100	110.9	104.5	98.0	96.1	100.0	106.3	113.8	114.6		
(percent change)		-5.7	-6.2	-2.0	4.1	6.3	7.1	0.7		
Adjustments from customs										
to BOP basis 1/	-143.3	-157.2	16.6	-295.3	-299.7	45.3	-328.0	416.0	416.0	416.0
Convertible currency										
exports, B.O.P.basis	4831.0	4832.0	4916.0	4188.0	4186.0	5051.0	5505.0	6446.0		
Imports, cif	4512.0	4453.4	4297.5	4353.7	4937.7	5386.7	5313.0	5476.0		
(percent change)		-1.3	-3.5	1.3	13.4	9.1	-1.4	3.1		
Imports, cif, 1986 prices	4474.8	4761.2	4776.1	4902.3	4937.7	5062.7	4715.2	4943.9		
(percent change)		6.4	0.4	2.6	0.7	2.5	-6.9	4.9		
Import prices, 1986=100	100.8	93.5	90.0	88.8	100.0	106.4	112.7	110.8		
(percent change)		-7.2	-3.8	-1.3	12.6	6.4	5.9	-1.7		
Adjustments from customs										
to BOP basis 1/	-349.0	-394.4	-272.5	-293.7	-269.7	-372.7	-297.0	434.0	434.0	434.0
Convertible currency										
imports, B.O.P.basis	4163.0	4059.0	4025.0	4060.0	4668.0	5014.0	5016.0	5910.0		
Terms of trade (US$)	109.9	111.7	108.9	108.2	100.0	99.9	101.0	103.5		
(percent change)		1.6	-2.5	-0.7	-7.5	-0.1	1.1	2.4		

Source: IMF Institute data base.

1/ Adjustments account for freight and insurance, leads and lags, and trade under clearing arrangements in currencies other than the ruble.

Table 5. Hungary: Exchange Rates and Exogenous Indicators 1/

	1982	1983	1984	1985	1986	1987	1988	1989	1990 1/	1991 1/	1992 1/	1993 1/	1994 1/
					(Percentage change, unless otherwise indicated)								
Ft/$, period average	36.631	42.671	48.042	50.119	45.832	46.971	50.413	59.066					
Ft/$, end of period	39.610	45.193	51.199	47.347	45.927	46.387	52.537	62.543					
$/SDR, period average	1.104	1.069	1.025	1.015	1.173	1.293	1.344	1.282	1.357	1.357	1.357	1.357	1.357
Partner GDP deflator (nat curr.)						2.8	2.8	3.6	3.8	3.4	3.1	3.0	2.9
Export markets 2/					3.3	3.4	4.2	3.3	2.9	2.7	2.7	2.8	2.8
Nonruble export prices (in U.S. dollars)		-5.7	-6.2	-2.0	4.1	6.3	7.1	0.7	5.0	3.8	2.9	4.1	4.1
Nonruble import prices (in U.S. dollars)		-7.2	-3.8	-1.3	12.6	6.4	5.9	-1.7	6.4	3.1	3.2	3.8	3.8
Interest rates LIBOR ($) 3/	13.69	10.18	11.82	9.11	6.95	7.61	8.41	9.31	8.45	9.00	9.25	9.00	8.75
Memorandum item: LIBOR (SDR) 4/	12.1	9.36	9.94	8.4	6.58	6.48	6.87	8.46	9.28				

Source: IMF Institute data base.

1/ Figures for 1990 and beyond are WEO and staff projections.
2/ Real domestic demand of trading partners.
3/ Rate on one year deposits denominated in U.S. dollars, period average.
4/ Rate on one year deposits denominated in SDRs, period average.

Table 6. Hungary: Commodity Composition of Nonruble Trade 1/

(In millions of U.S. dollars)

	1986	1987	1988	1989
Exports				
Energy products	137.9	150.0	186.4	202.8
Raw materials and semifinished products	1639.3	1930.7	2413.0	2671.3
Capital goods and transportation equipment	608.9	610.8	727.0	626.8
Industrial consumer goods	687.4	822.3	899.2	897.9
Food products	1129.8	1194.4	1475.1	1618.4
Total	4203.3	4708.2	5700.7	6017.2
Of which: Nonenergy	4065.4	4558.2	5514.3	5814.5
Imports				
Energy products	213.8	148.9	84.0	40.1
Raw materials and semifinished products	2683.8	2968.5	3282.5	3281.6
Capital goods and transportation equipment	658.1	751.3	716.2	943.6
Industrial consumer goods	583.5	615.7	534.1	645.0
Food products	532.8	543.4	565.0	552.5
Total	4672.0	5027.8	5181.8	5462.8
Of which: Nonenergy	4458.2	4878.9	5097.8	5422.7
Balance of trade				
Energy products	−75.8	1.0	102.4	162.7
Raw materials and semifinished products	−1044.5	−1037.7	−869.5	−610.3
Capital goods and transportation equipment	−49.2	−140.6	10.8	−316.8
Industrial consumer goods	103.9	206.6	365.0	252.9
Food products	597.0	650.9	910.1	1065.9
Total	−468.6	−319.8	518.8	554.4
Of which: Nonenergy	−392.8	−320.7	416.5	391.8

Source: IMF Institute data base.

1/ Exports are on an f.o.b. basis, imports on a c.i.f. basis.

Table 7. Hungary: Balance of Payments in Nonconvertible Currencies

(In millions of U.S. dollars)

	1982	1983	1984	1985	1986	1987	1988	1989	1990 Estimate
Trade balance	-258.0	-339.0	-111.0	320.0	17.0	43.0	94.0	507.0	194.0
Exports	4207.0	4146.0	4174.0	4390.0	5012.0	4916.0	4484.0	4047.0	2746.0
Imports	-4465.0	-4485.0	-4285.0	-4070.0	-4995.0	-4873.0	-4390.0	-3540.0	-2552.0
Services (net)	21.0	85.0	82.0	67.0	112.0	157.0	136.0	355.0	7.0
Freight and insurance, net	-91.0	-70.0	-65.0	-83.0	-76.0	-82.0	-77.0	-56.0	-10.0
Travel (net)	81.0	96.0	104.0	112.0	167.0	170.0	113.0	190.0	52.0
Credits	138.0	158.0	167.0	177.0	239.0	254.0	195.0	246.0	160.0
Debits	-57.0	-62.0	-63.0	-65.0	-72.0	-84.0	-82.0	-56.0	-108.0
Investment income (net)	5.0	-17.0	-34.0	-34.0	-28.0	-39.0	-16.0	-7.0	17.0
Credits	30.0	20.0	11.0	9.0	9.0	12.0	10.0	13.0	34.0
Debits	-25.0	-37.0	-45.0	-43.0	-37.0	-51.0	-26.0	-20.0	-17.0
Other current payments (net)	26.0	76.0	77.0	72.0	49.0	108.0	116.0	228.0	-52.0
Unrequited transfers (net)	2.0	3.0	3.0	4.0	4.0	3.0	2.0	4.0	53.0
Current account	-235.0	-251.0	-26.0	391.0	133.0	203.0	232.0	866.0	254.0
Medium- and long-term capital	96.0	100.0	15.0	-3.0	-215.0	-177.0	-268.0	-278.0	-98.0
Assets (net)	-18.0	8.0	-5.0	15.0	-48.0	-69.0	-69.0	-127.0	25.0
Liabilities (net)	114.0	92.0	20.0	-18.0	-167.0	-108.0	-199.0	-151.0	-123.0
Disbursements	133.0	131.0	182.0	54.0	66.0	59.0	44.0	20.0	12.0
Amortization	-19.0	-39.0	-162.0	-72.0	-233.0	-167.0	-243.0	-170.0	-135.0
Short-term capital (including errors and omissions)	180.0	128.0	3.0	-206.4	31.6	89.2	-51.5	-222.8	79.9
Capital account	276.0	238.0	24.0	-209.4	-183.4	-87.8	-319.5	-500.8	-18.1
Overall balance	41.0	-13.0	-2.0	181.6	-50.4	115.2	-87.5	365.2	235.9
Financing	-41.0	13.0	2.0	-181.6	50.4	-115.2	87.5	-365.2	-235.9
Change in reserves (inc.=-)	-40.0	13.0	2.0	-181.6	50.4	-115.2	87.5	-365.2	-235.9

Sources: IMF Institute data base.

131

Table 8. Hungary: Ruble Trade, Customs Basis

(In millions of U.S. dollars and percentage change)

	1984	1985	1986	1987	1988	1989	1990
Exports, fob	3685.9	4025.2	4675.5	4559.6	4124.8	3653.0	2517.0
(percent change)		9.2	16.2	−2.5	−9.5	−11.4	−31.1
Exports fob, 1986 prices	4323.3	4680.5	4675.5	4792.0	4820.5	4169.0	2775.4
(percent change)		8.3	−0.1	2.5	0.6	−13.5	−33.4
Export prices, 1986=100	85.3	86.0	100.0	95.2	85.6	87.6	90.7
(percent change)		0.9	16.3	−4.9	−10.1	2.4	3.5
Imports, cif	3805.5	3849.8	4654.7	4462.1	4040.4	3397.0	2518.0
(percent change)		1.2	20.9	−4.1	−9.5	−15.9	−25.9
Imports, cif, 1986 prices	4500.9	4484.2	4654.7	4826.5	5021.7	4163.7	3080.2
(percent change)		−0.4	3.8	3.7	4.0	−17.1	−26.0
Import prices, 1986=100	84.5	85.9	100.0	92.5	80.5	81.6	81.7
(percent change)		1.5	16.5	−7.6	−13.0	1.4	0.2
Terms of trade	100.8	100.2	100.0	102.9	106.3	107.4	110.9
(percent change)		−0.7	−0.2	2.9	3.3	1.0	3.3

Source: IMF Institute data base.

Table 9. Hungary: Commodity Composition of Ruble Trade 1/

(In millions of U.S. dollars)

	1986	1987	1988	1989
Exports				
Energy products	26.1	21.5	14.9	15.3
Raw materials and semifinished products	1041.6	997.1	893.4	852.7
Capital goods and transportation equipment	2147.3	2127.0	1922.3	1693.6
Industrial consumer goods	779.5	741.9	679.8	617.4
Food products	665.1	614.5	554.9	476.4
Total	4659.6	4502.0	4065.3	3655.4
Of which: Nonenergy	4633.4	4480.4	4050.3	3640.1
Imports				
Energy products	1489.2	1286.0	1101.6	934.6
Raw materials and semifinished products	1514.1	1486.9	1399.5	1200.8
Capital goods and transportation equipment	944.8	944.8	810.9	658.4
Industrial consumer goods	522.8	568.0	545.6	523.6
Food products	130.1	138.1	103.1	82.8
Total	4601.0	4423.8	3960.7	3400.2
Of which: Nonenergy	3111.8	3137.9	2859.0	2465.6
Balance of trade				
Energy products	−1463.1	−1264.5	−1086.7	−919.4
Raw materials and semifinished products	−472.6	−489.8	−506.1	−348.1
Capital goods and transportation equipment	1202.5	1182.1	1111.4	1035.2
Industrial consumer goods	256.7	173.8	134.2	93.8
Food products	535.0	476.4	451.8	393.6
Total	58.5	78.0	104.6	255.1
Of which: Nonenergy	1521.6	1342.5	1191.3	1174.5

Source: IMF Institute data base.

1/ Exports are on a f.o.b. basis and imports on a c.i.f. basis. Trade flows settled in rubles are converted from their forint value given in official statistics at the period U.S. dollar exchange rate.

Table 10. Hungary: Total Trade, Customs Basis 1/

(In millions of U.S. dollars and percentage change)

	1984	1985	1986	1987	1988	1989	1990
Exports, fob	8585.3	8508.5	9161.2	9565.3	9957.8	9683.0	...
(percent change)		−0.9	7.7	4.4	4.1	−2.8	...
Exports fob, 1986 prices	9321.5	9347.6	9161.2	9501.0	9944.0	9428.8	...
(percent change)		0.3	2.0	3.7	4.7	−5.2	...
Export prices, 1986=100	92.1	91.0	100.0	100.7	100.1	102.7	110.8
(percent change)		−1.2	9.9	0.7	−0.5	2.6	7.9
Imports, cif	8103.0	8203.5	9592.4	9848.8	9353.4	8873.0	...
(percent change)		1.2	16.9	2.7	−5.0	−5.1	...
Imports, cif, 1986 prices	9277.0	9386.5	9592.4	9889.2	9736.9	9107.7	...
(percent change)		1.2	2.2	3.1	−1.5	−6.5	...
Import prices, 1986=100	87.3	87.4	100.0	99.6	96.1	97.4	104.4
(percent change)		0.1	14.4	−0.4	−3.5	1.4	7.2
Terms of trade	105.4	104.1	100.0	101.1	104.2	105.4	106.2
(percent change)		−1.2	−4.0	1.1	3.1	1.1	0.7

Source: IMF Institute data base.

1/ Derived from Tables 4 and 8.

134

Table 11. Hungary: Outstanding External Debt

(In millions of U.S. dollars, at end of period)

	1982	1983	1984	1985	1986	1987	1988	1989
Total external debt	11,515	12,125	12,216	15,106	17,928	20,531	20,150	20,966
In convertible currencies	10,216	10,746	10,983	13,955	16,907	19,584	19,603	20,605
By original maturity								
Short-term	3,261	3,904	2,977	3,019	3,494	3,103	3,363	3,306
Medium- and long-term	6,955	6,842	8,006	10,936	13,413	16,481	16,240	17,299
By type of credit:								
Financial loans	9,155	9,208	9,428	12,175	15,084	17,508	17,469	18,060
Trade-related credits	661	1,144	1,125	1,318	1,433	1,652	1,626	1,763
Intergovernment credits	5	4	3	2	1	0	--	--
Other	396	390	428	459	389	422	508	568
In nonconvertible currencies	1,299	1,379	1,233	1,151	1,021	947	547	361
By original maturity								
Short-term	250	367	916	106	111	184	120	87
Medium- and long-term	1,049	1,012	317	1,045	910	763	427	274
By type of credit:								
Financial loans	251	366	313	133	140	210	136	88
Trade-related credits	39	30	24	0	--	--	--	--
Intergovernment credits	974	948	863	1,009	873	728	438	260
Other	35	38	32	8	8	8	8	12
Memorandum item:								
Convertible currency debt 1/								
(as percent of GDP)	44.1	51.1	53.9	67.7	71.2	75.0	70.1	70.3

Source: IMF Institute data base

1/ End of period convertible currency external debt divided by GDP for the year as a whole in local currency units and converted into U.S. Dollars at the period average forint/U.S. Dollar exchange rate.

Table 12. Hungary: External Debt Service in Convertible Currencies

	1982	1983	1984	1985	1986	1987	1988	1989
				(In millions of U.S. dollars)				
Total debt service	2,432	2,351	2,705	3,689	4,182	3,747	3,510	3,569
a. Principal	1235	1496	1761	2670	2967	2524	2204	1964
Excluding Fund repurchases	1,235	1,496	1,761	2,580	2,919	2,170	1,849	1,740
Fund repurchases	0	0	0	90	48	354	355	224
b. Interest	1,197	855	944	1,019	1,215	1,223	1,306	1,605
				(In percent)				
Total debt service 1/	47.0	45.4	51.0	79.2	87.1	64.2	54.8	48.2
a. Principal								
Excluding Fund repurchases	23.9	28.9	33.2	55.4	60.8	37.2	28.9	23.5
Fund repurchases	0.0	0.0	0.0	1.9	1.0	6.1	5.5	3.0
b. Interest	23.1	16.5	17.8	21.9	25.3	20.9	20.4	21.7

Source: IMF Institute data base.

1/ As percent of merchandise exports, and travel and income credits.

Table 13. Hungary: Principal Obligations in Convertible Currencies on End–1989 Debt, 1990–94

(In millions of U.S. dollars)

	1990	1991	1992	1993	1994
Principal	2,062	2,407	2,542	2,229	2,396
Fund repurchases	322	79	46	51	254
Debts disbursed before 1990	1,740	2,328	2,496	2,178	2,142

Source: IMF Institute data base.

Table 14. Hungary: Medium-Term Balance of Payments and External Debt Projections

I. EXOGENOUS ASSUMPTIONS 1/

	1991	1992	1993	1994
	(Percentage change unless otherwise indicated)			
External				
Exports	1.10	1.10	1.10	1.10
Imports	1.08	1.08	1.08	1.08
Investment income credits	1.10	1.10	1.10	1.10
Travel credits	1.10	1.10	1.10	1.10
Other services (net)	1.05	1.05	1.05	1.05
Unrequited transfers (net)	1.10	1.10	1.10	1.10
Net direct investment	1.10	1.10	1.10	1.10
Short-term capital inflows	1.10	1.10	1.10	1.10
Reserve target (in months of imports, end of period)	3.5	3.5	3.5	3.5
Interest rate (US$, in percent)	0.0900	0.0925	0.0900	0.0875
Domestic				
GDP at 1986 prices	1.025	1.025	1.025	1.025
Memorandum item:				
Partner GDP deflator (US$)	1.034	1.031	1.030	1.029

1/ Summary of worksheet inputs.

Table 14. Hungary: Medium-Term Balance of Payments and External Debt Projections (continued)

II. MEDIUM-TERM BALANCE OF PAYMENTS PROJECTIONS

	1990	1991	1992	1993	1994
	(In millions of U.S. dollars)				
Exports	6400.0	7040.0	7744.0	8518.4	9370.2
Imports	-6382.0	-6892.6	-7444.0	-8039.5	-8682.6
Services (net)	-2297.5	-2581.6	-2843.3	-3031.0	-3261.1
Investment income (net)	-1597.5	-1887.1	-2158.8	-2361.4	-2612.1
Credits	233.0	256.3	281.9	310.1	341.1
Debits	-1830.5	-2143.4	-2440.7	-2671.6	-2953.2
On end-1989 long- and medium-term debt	-1388.3	-1295.6	-1108.4	-868.1	-655.0
On post-1989 long- and medium-term debt	-163.9	-541.0	-990.7	-1441.1	-1922.6
On short-term debt	-278.4	-306.9	-341.6	-362.4	-375.6
Travel credits	811.8	893.0	982.3	1080.5	1188.6
Other services (net)	-1511.8	-1587.4	-1666.8	-1750.1	-1837.6
Unrequited transfers (net)	130.0	143.0	157.3	173.0	190.3
Current Account	-2149.5	-2291.1	-2385.9	-2379.1	-2383.2
Direct investment	200.0	220.0	242.0	266.2	292.8
Other medium- and long-term capital (net)	2138.5	1938.2	1987.8	1938.3	2092.7
Disbursements	3878.5	4266.2	5130.2	5473.7	6447.2
Amortization	1740.0	2328.0	3142.4	3535.4	4354.5
Of end-1989 debt	1740.0	2328.0	2496.0	2178.0	2142.0
Of post-1989 debt	0.0	0.0	646.4	1357.4	2212.5
Short-term capital	300.0	330.0	363.0	399.3	439.2
Capital Account	2638.5	2488.2	2592.8	2603.8	2824.8
Overall Balance	489.0	197.1	206.8	224.7	441.6
Financing	-489.0	-197.1	-206.8	-224.7	-441.6
Change in reserves	-167.0	-118.1	-160.8	-173.7	-187.6
Use of Fund credit	-322.0	-79.0	-46.0	-51.0	-254.0
Purchases					
Repurchases	-322.0	-79.0	-46.0	-51.0	-254.0
Memorandum items:					
International reserves (end period) 1/	1892.3	2010.3	2171.2	2344.8	2532.4
GDP (in millions of U.S. dollars)	31017.3	32873.6	34740.0	36676.8	38683.9

1/ Net international reserves in convertible currencies at end-1989 were US$ 1,725.3 million.

Table 14. Hungary: Medium–Term Balance of Payments and External Debt Projections (continued)

III. SUMMARY OF EXTERNAL INDICATORS

	1990	1991	1992	1993	1994
Current account (percent of GDP)	–6.9	–7.0	–6.9	–6.5	–6.2
Total outstanding debt (percent of GDP) 1/	73.3	75.8	80.2	85.9	93.1
Total outstanding debt (percent of merchandise exports, travel and income credits) 1/	305.2	304.2	309.3	318.0	330.2
Debt service (percent of merchandise exports, travel and income credits)	48.0	54.6	62.0	62.6	67.0
Interest payments (percent of merchandise exports, travel and income credits)	24.6	26.2	27.1	27.0	27.1

1/ Outstanding debt as of end of period.

Table 14. Hungary: Medium–Term Balance of Payments and External Debt Projections (concluded)

IV. WORKING TABLE A: DERIVATION OF PRINCIPAL AND INTEREST PAYMENTS ON MEDIUM–TERM EXTERNAL DEBT

	1990	1991	1992	1993	1994
1. Disbursements	3878.5	4266.2	5130.2	5473.7	6447.2
2. Amortization of pre-1989 debt	1740.0	2328.0	2496.0	2178.0	2142.0
3. Amortization of post-1989 debt	0.0	0.0	646.4	1357.4	2212.5
On 1990 flows	0.0	0.0	646.4	646.4	646.4
On 1991 flows	0.0	0.0	0.0	711.0	711.0
On 1992 flows	0.0	0.0	0.0	0.0	855.0
On 1993 flows	0.0	0.0	0.0	0.0	0.0
On 1994 flows	0.0	0.0	0.0	0.0	0.0
4. Total outstanding debt	19437.5	21375.7	24009.9	27305.6	31610.8
End-1989 debt 1/	15559.0	13231.0	10735.0	8557.0	6415.0
Post-1989 debt	3878.5	8144.7	13274.9	18748.6	25195.8
5. Total interest payments	1552.1	1836.6	2099.1	2309.2	2577.6
On end-1989 debt	1388.3	1295.6	1108.4	868.1	655.0
On post-1989 debt	163.9	541.0	990.7	1441.1	1922.6
Memorandum items					
Total medium-term debt service	3292.1	4164.6	5241.5	5844.6	6932.1
Principal	1740.0	2328.0	3142.4	3535.4	4354.5
Prior to 1990	1740.0	2328.0	2496.0	2178.0	2142.0
After 1990	0.0	0.0	646.4	1357.4	2212.5
Interest	1552.1	1836.6	2099.1	2309.2	2577.6
Prior to 1990	1388.3	1295.6	1108.4	868.1	655.0
After 1990	163.9	541.0	990.7	1441.1	1922.6

V. WORKING TABLE B: DERIVATION OF INTEREST PAYMENTS ON TOTAL SHORT–TERM DEBT

	1990	1991	1992	1993	1994
1. Disbursements	300.0	330.0	363.0	399.3	439.2
2. Fund repurchases (net)	-322.0	-79.0	-46.0	-51.0	-254.0
3. Debt outstanding end-year 2/	3284.0	3535.0	3852.0	4200.3	4385.5
4. Interest on total short-term debt	278.4	306.9	341.6	362.4	375.6

1/ Medium-and long-term debt outstanding at end-1989 was US$ 17,299 million.

2/ Short-term debt outstanding at end-1989 was US$ 3,306 million.

141

VI.   Fiscal Sector

The Role of Government and Fiscal Reform in an Economy in Transition 1/

1. Definition of the government and the public sector

The government sector is generally defined to encompass the authorities that are engaged in the pursuit of public purposes by providing nonmarket services and effecting income transfers financed by levies on other sectors in the economy. 2/ These functions are performed by all entities of the *general government* sector, which mainly comprise: (1) the central government; (2) state governments; and (3) local governments. Social security funds and departmental enterprises 3/ are also included in the definition of the general government and are treated as belonging to the level of government at which they operate. Government-owned or controlled financial institutions are classified as public financial institutions, however, rather than as part of general government.

In market economies, nonfinancial public enterprises that produce and sell goods and services are excluded from the government sector but included in the definition of the *public sector*. Such enterprises represent government-owned or public utilities and other nationalized or government established enterprises. In the context of centrally planned economies, these enterprises may represent the dominant part of the productive sector of the economy, intended to play a similar role in the supply of goods and services as private enterprises in a market economy. It may, therefore, not be of significant analytical benefit to use the definition of the public sector in these economies.

The definition of general government outlined above essentially applies to both centrally planned and market economies. A closer scrutiny reveals, however, significant differences between the two systems as regards the role of government, the institutional structure of the government sector, and the instruments employed in the interaction of government with the other sectors of the economy.

In market economies, with the private sector playing a leading role in promoting economic growth and the public sector designed to provide a stable and supportive environment, fiscal policy is focused on the achievement of macroeconomic stability, allocative efficiency, and distributional equity consistent with prevailing social preferences. In centrally planned economies, the government sector assumed to a far larger extent direct responsibility for the control of economic processes.

1/ This chapter draws on the IBRD Country Economic Memorandum, "Hungary: Reform and Decentralization of the Public Sector," Annex II, "Fiscal Structure and Developments in Hungary," forthcoming.

2/ See IMF, Manual on Government Finance Statistics, p. 7.

3/ Departmental enterprises perform specific services for the government sector; they encompass printing and publishing, restaurants in public buildings, and dwellings for government employees.

Such control was exercised in pursuit of a development strategy that involved a large scale mobilization of resources to promote rapid industrialization dominated by a heavy industrial sector. The government further implemented an ambitious program of resource transfers to achieve an egalitarian distribution of income and consumption in society, consistent with the priorities established by the political leadership.

The enhanced role of government in controlling resource allocation was reflected in a pervasive presence of government in the economy through specific institutions, such as central planning agencies, boards for the control of prices, wages, and foreign trade, and branch ministries administering a large state enterprise sector. Institutions that provide legal, regulatory, and administrative services to support the efficient operation of markets were essentially absent. The specific emphasis on the allocative and redistributive responsibilities of government and the priorities underlying the development strategy pursued under socialist central planning led to a large scale intermediation of resources through the budget, raising the share of government expenditures in GDP by 10–15 percent above the typical level in major market economies. These factors also determined the structure of government expenditures and revenues. The composition of expenditures was heavily weighted in favor of subsidies and transfers. The bulk of revenues stemmed from receipts from profits, payroll taxes, and turnover taxes while revenues from individual income taxes remained low by international standards.

The tax structure was marked by a considerable disregard for efficiency. High profit tax receipts were facilitated by an inflation of enterprise residual income through unrealistic amortization rules, very low interest rates paid to enterprises, and, especially, tightly controlled wages. Wages from the socialized sector were divorced from the marginal productivity of labor, as they were supplemented at the household level by extensive social benefits in kind, intermediated through the government sector. This practice drove a significant wedge between factor incomes and disposable incomes and thus between the social and private return on effort, with adverse consequences for economic efficiency.

In centrally planned economies, it was largely the prerogative of the plan to carry out the role played by the price system in market economies. Taxes, and especially those on profits, represented a primary instrument to enforce the plan. As a result, profit taxes were highly differentiated and the tax parameters were frequently adjusted in response to the diverse and changing priorities of the plan. Such taxes were in practice often quite arbitrary and the result of a bargaining process between enterprises and the fiscal authorities, typically effecting a redistribution of resources from efficient to inefficient enterprises.

The scope for income taxation was limited by the low level of socialized sector wages and the consideration that the primary distribution of such labor income was adequate and required no further correction. Schedular income taxes were mainly used to impose prohibitive tax rates on incomes of artists and self-employed professionals and craftsmen in order to bring such incomes closer in line with those from the socialized sector and to contain private sector economic activities.

The above differences between centrally planned and market economies manifest themselves to some degree also in the various stages of transition in which formerly centrally planned economies find themselves in the process of transformation to market economies. Thus, they may have an important bearing on the size of the government sector, the forecasting of budget aggregates, and the design and conduct of fiscal policy in the transition period.

2. Fiscal reforms in Hungary and fiscal developments in 1989

a. Hungarian fiscal reforms

Economic reforms undertaken in Hungary since the early 1950s also encompassed various efforts to modify the role of fiscal policy. During the initial period of traditional central planning the budget was an instrument to enforce plan implementation through massive ad hoc transfers of resources among state enterprises and a large scale redistribution of incomes among households.

The most comprehensive attempt at market-oriented reform in a centrally planned economy was initiated with the introduction of the New Economic Mechanism (NEM) in Hungary in 1968. The NEM was aimed at replacing direct by indirect control over socialized enterprises with limited financial self management. This method was intended to achieve the priorities set out in the national economic plans with greater efficiency. The fiscal reform measures mainly involved the adoption of nominally parametric fiscal instruments to redistribute profits in pursuit of production, trade, income, and price policy objectives as well as a streamlining of the complex system of price subsidies and turnover taxes; more than 2,500 implicit rates were replaced by about 1,000 explicit turnover tax rates.

A significant step was also taken to rationalize the fiscal regime with respect to international trade, in conjunction with a reform of the exchange system. The multitude of exchange rates, which had been highly differentiated through a complex system of price equalization taxes and subsidies, was transformed into a system of unified exchange rates vis-à-vis the nonruble and the ruble areas, respectively. For trade with the nonruble area, the former complex fiscal regime was replaced by an import tariff system with a wide dispersion of rates. Since foreign trade remained subject to considerable direct control, however, the import duties became primarily an instrument of bargaining for trade concessions with nonruble trading partners. With respect to the ruble area, a system of nonparametric "producers' differential turnover taxes" was applied to bridge the gap between the rather arbitrary prices applied in ruble trade transactions—converted at the unified forint/ruble exchange rate—and Hungarian domestic prices that were linked to a substantial degree to world market prices. 1/

1/ In addition to imports from the ruble area, the producers' differential turnover tax was also levied on a number of domestic products, notably energy, whose domestic prices were higher than production costs.

In the course of the 1970s, especially following the sharp rise of petroleum and other raw material prices beginning in 1973, fiscal intervention again became more pervasive and discretionary. Various new production taxes and tax preferences were introduced in an effort to insulate the domestic economy from a full pass through of price developments in the world markets. The complexity of the tax system was exacerbated by a strong differentiation of the fiscal measures among branches and even individual enterprises.

A renewed effort to simplify that tax system was undertaken in conjunction with a comprehensive price reform introduced in 1980. The latter reforms initiated a shift in the burden of taxation from the factors of production to profits, as production taxes were lowered and the 5 percent charge on the state owned capital of enterprises was rescinded, while profit tax rates were raised.

The gains in transparency and predictability of fiscal instruments were eroded again, however, in the following period, by frequent tax adjustments and a confiscatory withdrawal of past retained earnings from enterprises. The latter revenues were allocated through the budget and extra budgetary funds to supporting weak enterprises in crisis industries and in areas of economic decline. The complexity of the system was further enhanced by the introduction of new taxes on the wage bill and the profits of enterprises and an anti-cyclical investment tax in 1985. These and other steps also brought about a reversal of the earlier shift of the burden of taxation from factors of production to profits.

Although a significant step to simplify the structure of turnover taxes was also intended by the authorities in the framework of the 1985 tax reforms, the effort actually implemented fell considerably short of original plans. Thus, the fiscal system in place in the mid-1980s continued to be marked by multiple taxation with multiple aims, violating the general principle of neutrality, transparency, stability, and equity of taxation.

A broad overhaul of the system was initiated subsequently, to be implemented during 1988-89. In a first phase, a value added tax—called a *general turnover tax* (GTT)—and a *personal income tax* (PIT) were adopted at the beginning of 1988. The contemporaneous elimination or modification of other taxes, including the municipal contribution on profits, the net worth tax, the investment tax, and wage taxes paid by socialized enterprises, affected about 90 percent of general government revenue, leaving essentially unchanged only taxes on international trade. The GTT replaced the multitude of existing turnover taxes. The tax base of the GTT was defined narrowly, excluding food, basic services, construction materials, personal imports, and other items and the GTT was fully rebated on exports. As a consequence, rates were set high by international standards. They encompassed a standard rate of 25 percent, which yielded 95 percent of GTT revenue, and a reduced rate of 15 percent; a zero rate applied to goods accounting for more than 40 percent of consumer expenditures; a rebate on investment expenditures of socialized enterprises was to be phased in gradually during 1988-92.

The PIT superseded a complex system of schedular income taxes with high statutory marginal rates on incomes from self-employment and intellectual and cultural activities. For the first time, a taxation of wages earned by individuals in the socialized sector and of interest income was established. With the introduction of the PIT, socialized sector wages were grossed-up to preserve the net income of employees. The tax burden on incomes from private economic activities became heavier as the new income tax was applied on aggregate income at the applicable marginal rate, instead of a separate taxation of incomes from different sources under the previous schedular income tax regime and an additional 25 percent entrepreneurial tax was imposed on the profits of private undertakings. The initial PIT rates ranged from 20 percent to 60 percent. About 20 percent of potential taxpayers were expected to fall below the threshold of a general tax-free allowance, equivalent to about two thirds of average earnings in the socialized sector. An additional allowance was granted to employees as a lump sum cost deduction in lieu of itemized expense accounting. Exemptions were applicable to incomes from small scale farming and intellectual activities and most social benefits; interest income on domestic currency financial assets was subjected to a separate flat rate withholding tax of 20 percent; and generous provisions were granted for the deductibility of savings for housing purposes and interest on housing loans. As a result, the PIT was levied on only about one half of household incomes. In 1989, the top marginal tax rate was lowered to 56 percent while brackets were widened and their number reduced to 8; the tax base was also narrowed further.

With the adoption of the PIT, *social security contribution* rates of employees were changed from a progressive schedule of 3–15 percent to a unified rate of 10 percent and employers' contribution rates outside the government sector were revised to 43 percent. Moreover, the new contribution rates were applied to the grossed up wages of employees in the socialized sector including the incidence of the PIT. In 1989, employers' contribution rates in the government sector were also raised to the unified rate of 43 percent (from a previous rate of 10 percent) and social security transactions were moved from the state budget to a separate Social Insurance Fund (SIF). At the same time, a formal unemployment compensation fund was introduced and the subsidization of housing finance was moved from the banking sector to a new housing fund, whose losses are covered by transfers from the state budget. 1/

The second major step toward a more efficient tax system was taken with the rationalization of profit taxation through the adoption of the *enterprise profit tax* (EPT) at the beginning of 1989. The EPT substituted the previous highly differentiated profit tax as well as taxes levied on incomes of private enterprises. At the same time, several production taxes in metallurgy, the chemical industry, transportation, and public services were also removed. The general EPT rate was initially set at 50 percent, with a temporary surcharge of 4 percent and a reduced rate of 40 percent levied on the first Ft 3 million tranche of taxable profit to favor small businesses. The marginal effective tax rate of the EPT was high by international standards, partly because the tax base was severely narrowed down by

---

1/ The transfer of housing loan subsidies to the budget removed a disturbing quasi-fiscal function from the Savings Bank, which had represented a formidable obstacle in the way of efforts to complete the reform of the banking system (see Chapter VII).

several tax preferences maintained for farming, food processing, various services, cultural activities, and especially for joint ventures with foreign partners.

b. Fiscal developments in 1989

The intermediation of resources through the budget in Hungary—at over 60 percent of GDP—has been very high by the standards of major European market economies (see Table 1). In line with the discussion of the specific role of government under socialist central planning in the preceding section, the large share of government in GDP has been chiefly attributable to high transfer payments for subsidies to enterprises and income maintenance programs for households. Together these have accounted for about one third of GDP and one half of government expenditures (Table 2). As the need to restore macroecomomic stability has placed a tight constraint on the allowable budget deficit, a significant effort had to be undertaken by the authorities to mobilize revenue through taxation. These conditions, together with the narrow base of the new taxes, played an important role in the decision to set the initial rates of the GTT and the PIT in 1988 higher·than originally contemplated.

Table 1. Hungary: General Government Accounts

(In percent of GDP)

	Hungary		EC Average	
	1985	1989	1985	1989
Revenue	60	59	44	44
Individual income tax	1	5	9	9
Enterprise income taxes and transfers	16	14	5	4
Social security contributions	13	17	13	13
Taxes on goods and services	20	21	11	11
Other revenue	8	2	6	7
Total expenditure	61	60	48	46
Current expenditure	53	54	44	42
Goods and services	19	20	17	16
Interest	–	2	5	5
Subsidies and transfers	34	31	19	18
Capital expenditure	8	6	4	4
Overall balance	-1	-1	-4	-3

Sources: IMF, Institute data base and G. Kopits, Fiscal Reform in European Economies in Transition, WP/91/43, April 1991; and Fund staff estimates.

Table 2. Hungary: General Government Operations

(in percent of GDP)

	1982	1983	1984	1985	1986	1987	1988	1989 Plan	1989 Outturn
Revenue	59.2	60.9	60.8	60.0	61.5	59.1	63.4	58.1	58.9
Tax Revenue	49.6	52.9	52.6	49.9	52.2	52.4	54.0	51.3	48.3
Of which:									
Individual income taxes	0.5	0.9	0.9	0.9	0.8	0.8	4.7	4.9	5.4
Enterprise income taxes 1/	12.1	13.1	12.6	9.6	11.1	11.9	8.4	8.7	6.9
Payroll taxes	8.9	9.4	12.0	15.7	16.6	15.5	14.4	13.8	14.1
Taxes on goods and services	24.6	24.9	21.4	19.8	20.2	19.7	25.7	23.4	21.3
Nontax revenue 2/	9.6	8.0	8.2	10.1	9.2	6.7	9.4	6.8	10.6
Total expenditure 3/	61.2	61.9	59.4	61.1	64.6	62.7	63.3	57.8	60.2
Current expenditure	51.9	53.5	51.5	53.2	56.6	54.6	55.6	52.4	53.7
Goods and services	19.1	17.9	17.7	18.7	19.4	19.5	21.5	19.5	20.2
Interest	1.1	0.2	0.6	0.4	1.3	2.6	1.6	0.8	2.4
Subsidies and transfers	31.7	35.4	33.2	34.1	35.8	32.4	32.5	32.0	31.1
Capital expenditure 3/	9.3	8.4	7.9	7.9	8.0	8.1	7.7	5.4	6.5
Overall balance	-2.1	-1.1	1.4	-1.1	-3.1	-3.5	--	0.4	-1.3
Financing	2.1	1.1	-1.4	1.1	3.1	3.5	--	-0.4	1.3
External financing	0.3	0.5	0.1	-0.1	-0.3	-0.6	-0.6	-0.6	-0.6
Domestic financing	1.7	0.6	-1.5	1.2	3.9	4.2	0.6	0.2	1.9
Nonbank borrowing	...	0.1	-0.4	1.0	-1.4	0.1	--	...	-1.3
Bank borrowing, net	...	0.5	-1.1	0.3	5.4	4.1	0.5	...	3.2

Source: IMF Institute data base.

1/ Including profit transfers from government-owned financial and nonfinancial enterprises.
2/ Including capital revenue.
3/ Including a small amount of lending less repayments.

Fiscal policy for 1989 was geared to reducing the scope of government intervention, while contributing further to a containment of external imbalances. The authorities launched a medium-term program to curtail transfers to the enterprise and household sectors and planned to reduce government investment and defense outlays, measures that were expected to lower the share of government expenditures in GDP by over 5 percentage points. As the general government overall balance was targeted to record a slight surplus (0.4 percent of GDP) and nontax revenues were expected to weaken with sluggish economic activity, the authorities saw only a moderate scope—amounting to about 3 percent of GDP—for an easing of the tax burden on the economy. Revenue losses were anticipated from a lowering of the PIT rates by an average of 3 percentage points, the scheduled widening of the GTT rebate for investment goods, and a decline in receipts from the differential producers' turnover tax, mainly attributable to rising ruble import prices. A marked increase was planned, however, in receipts from the taxation of enterprise profits, given the high initial tax rates applied under the newly adopted EPT and the 4 percent surtax added for 1989.

The outturn of general government operations was less satisfactory than planned. Targeted expenditures were overshot—despite a further cut of defense outlays at mid-year—owing in part to the effect of higher than anticipated inflation on spending on goods and services and—through firming interest rates—on interest payments on government debt. A marked shift took place in the structure of central government subsidies, as the cuts in consumer and producer subsidies as well as support to agriculture and CMEA exports were largely offset by a sharp rise in housing loan subsidies, which had been assumed by the budget from the banking system (Table 3).

The expenditure overruns in 1989 were not fully matched by stronger than planned revenues. A surge was recorded in nontax revenues, but extra revenues collected by certain budgetary institutions were used for higher capital expenditures, conflicting with the intent of the government to scale down the scope of fiscal intermediation. The collection of tax revenues was markedly lower than planned, due to a significant shortfall of profit tax receipts. EPT revenue was 40 percent lower than expected, partly because profits were squeezed by larger than anticipated wage increases, but more importantly because tax reliefs and refunds granted to state companies and the accumulation of arrears to the government by enterprises in financial distress had been significantly underestimated.

A further shortfall occurred in the producers' differential turnover tax as the volume of ruble imports fell markedly. The latter shortfall was not mitigated by higher revenue that could have been obtained from an unanticipated surge in private consumption and convertible currency imports in 1989, as buoyant expenditures largely reflected personal imports of consumer durables, which were both exempt from the GTT and subject to a relaxed regime of customs duties. Thus, despite an increase of petroleum excises at mid-year for budgetary considerations, revenue from goods and services also remained below target.

Table 3. Hungary: General Government Current Subsidies and Transfers

(in percent of GDP)

	1982	1983	1984	1985	1986	1987	1988	1989 Plan	1989 Outturn
Central government subsidies	17.8	18.9	15.7	15.5	15.9	15.6	13.2	10.9	12.0
Consumer subsidies	7.6	7.4	5.5	4.9	5.5	5.4	3.2	2.5	2.5
Producer subsidies	2.1	2.0	1.5	1.3	1.5	1.3	1.0	0.4	0.3
Agricultural support	1.1	2.0	1.3	1.5	1.3	1.2	1.1	0.6	0.7
Tax rebate to exporters	1.7	1.3	1.1	1.3	2.0	2.0	1.3	1.0	1.3
CMEA price equalization	3.1	3.4	3.5	3.7	3.8	4.2	4.1	3.0	2.5
Import subsidies and other	1.7	1.9	2.1	2.1	1.1	0.7	0.7	0.2	0.5
Housing loan subsidies	0.6	0.7	0.7	0.7	0.8	0.8	1.8	3.3	4.0
Central government transfers	13.0	15.8	16.7	17.1	19.3	16.5	18.6	20.5	18.6
Social security pensions	8.1	8.4	8.6	8.5	9.1	9.0	9.2	9.5	9.0
Other social security benefits	3.5	3.6	3.6	4.2	3.9	3.6	6.1	6.5	6.5
Other current transfers	1.4	3.8	4.5	4.3	6.2	3.9	3.3	4.5	3.0
Local government subsidies	0.8	0.8	0.7	1.6	0.7	0.6	0.7	0.5	0.5
Current subsidies and transfers	31.7	35.4	33.2	34.1	35.8	32.7	32.5	32.0	31.1

Source: IMF Institute data base.

The overall shortfall of tax revenue was tempered, however, by excess receipts from the PIT and social security contributions stemming from sharp overruns of wage increases in socialized enterprises following a liberalization of the wage system and an easing of credit conditions.

Instead of the anticipated small surplus, the overall position of the general government closed with a deficit of over 1 percent of GDP in 1989. In addition, the government had to mobilize resources to finance a continued redemption of official debt to the USSR, equivalent to just over 0.5 percent of GDP in 1989.

In meeting these requirements, the Treasury encountered serious financing difficulties. The placement of government bonds and Treasury bills was hampered by an increasing preference of the public for shares and consumer durables, in light of rising inflationary expectations. In effect, nonbank investors reduced their holdings of government paper during the year. As a result, the government resorted to renewed central bank financing on a significant scale, equivalent to about 3 percent of GDP. This amounted essentially to an onlending of funds borrowed in the international financial markets by the National Bank of Hungary, which has been chiefly responsible for official borrowing from the convertible currency area.

Forecasting Government Transactions

Government operations have a significant impact on the economy, reflecting the size and structure of revenues and expenditures as well as the magnitude and financing of the budget balance. Domestic absorption is affected directly through government expenditures on goods and services and indirectly through the effects of revenues and expenditures on private spending. 1/ Owing to the central role of the budget, fiscal developments have in many instances been the chief cause of major internal and external economic imbalances. Consequently, the assessment and forecasting of government transactions represent key elements in the design of stabilization and adjustment programs.

The following section reviews the general forecasting methods for tax revenues, nontax revenues, government expenditures, and the financing of the budget balance and discusses issues related to the practical application of the pertinent techniques in the case of Hungary and other economies in transition.

1. General methodology of forecasting government transactions

a. Tax revenue

Constraints on data availability may sometimes lead to forecasting tax revenues by an extrapolation of recent trends. Such estimates are not very robust, however, because they assume that revenues will merely reproduce past developments regardless of the evolution of the tax base or the tax system. More reliable forecasts require, therefore, methods that link tax revenues to their bases. In principle, such revenue forecasts should allow for a feedback between taxes and their bases, because changes in tax parameters will affect behaviors that influence the aggregates on which the taxes are levied. Taking into account such linkages requires, however, the construction of a comprehensive econometric model, for which, in may instances, adequate data and other resources may not be available. A more practical approach, called the *partial equilibrium* approach, is to project revenues on the basis of functions for different types of taxes, assuming given projections of the tax bases.

The development of tax functions requires decisions on the degree of *disaggregation* and the choice of appropriate *proxy tax bases*. The breakdown should attempt to distinguish between the major tax categories. Also, a group of taxes should be disaggregated if their bases are quite dissimilar. However, very detailed breakdowns of revenue will increase the likelihood of fluctuations of an increasingly

---

1/ Government revenues and expenditures also affect economic growth through their influence on the mobilization of savings and the allocation of capital and labor.

random character. A balance must be struck, therefore, between these conflicting considerations.

After the appropriate revenue classification is selected, consideration needs to be given to the approximation of the tax bases. In principle, each category could be related to the legal base as defined by the tax law. Data on the legal base are, however, often unavailable in a usable form. The revenue classification may also have grouped in a single category taxes subject to different rates or applied to different legal bases. Consequently, an alternative to the legal base is often required. Since major tax categories often relate to the bases that cover large parts of overall economic activity, alternative or proxy bases may be found among the variables comprising the national accounts and the balance of payments. The selection of the most appropriate proxy base will in part depend on whether projections for such variables are generated in other parts of the financial programming exercise. If the latter aggregates are determined in the context of a financial program, a sequential procedure can be employed whereby the tax revenue implications of different base solutions are examined in order to ensure a consistent interaction among macroeconomic variables.

An increase in revenue over a particular period can reflect both *automatic* and *discretionary* effects. The former represents the rise in revenue that stems from the growth in the tax base. Discretionary changes in revenue result from modifications of the tax system, including a revision of existing tax rates, a change in the coverage of a tax, or the introduction of a new tax. Analysis and forecasting of revenue developments generally require a distinction between these automatic and discretionary components. A simple method to eliminate the effects of discretionary measures on the growth rate of actual revenues—the proportional adjustment method—is briefly reviewed in Box 1.

The distinction between the automatic and discretionary effects leads to two different concepts for summarizing the response of a tax to developments in the economy. *Buoyancy* is defined as the ratio of the percentage change in actual tax collections over the data period to the percentage change in GDP. In order to concentrate on just the automatic effects on revenue, however, the alternative concept of *elasticity* has been developed. Elasticity compares the growth in revenue with the rise in GDP on the assumption that the tax system of a particular year (usually the most recent) had prevailed throughout the period (see Box 2). The interpretation of the size of the elasticity is similar to that for buoyancy with the important difference that it reflects only the automatic response of revenue. Thus, for an observation period in which discretionary changes in the tax system would have yielded an increase in revenue collections, the tax elasticity would be exceeded by the tax buoyancy, which would overstate the automatic response of revenue to a given change in GDP.

Following an adjustment of actual revenue series for the effects of discretionary measures, the major step in the procedure to forecast tax revenues would consist of specifying functional relationships between the adjusted revenue series and the

156

Proportional Adjustment Method

Based of information on actual tax revenue (T) and the estimated revenue effect of discretionary measures (D) — the proportional adjustment method allows the derivation of an adjusted revenue (AT) series that approximates the amounts of taxes that would have been paid in prior years if the tax system of the base year (t) had been in force throughout the period. A key assumption is that a given discretionary tax change would have the same proportionate effect on tax receipts in all years. The adjustment procedure can be illustrated by the following formulae:

(1) $\quad AT_t = T_t$

since, by definition, no revenue adjustment applies for the base year

(2) $\quad AT_{t-1} = T_{t-1} \left[\dfrac{T_t}{T_t - D_t} \right]$

Substituting (1) into (2):

(3) $\quad AT_{t-1} = T_{t-1} \left[\dfrac{AT_t}{T_t - D_t} \right]$

In general, for any period t-n equation (3) can be written as:

(4) $\quad AT_{t-n} = T_{t-n} \left[\dfrac{AT_{t-n+1}}{T_{t-n+1} - D_{t-n+1}} \right]$

Box 1

assumed tax base, estimating a set of parameters that characterize the current tax structure, and applying the estimated equations to forecasting revenues for given projections of the tax bases. 1/ If adequate information is not available, more simple alternative methods can be used whose results would be less reliable than those of the above forecasting procedure but still superior to a simple extrapolation of trends. Revenue projections would be prepared by relating tax categories to pertinent macroeconomic variables and making assumptions about factors that might affect the revenue ratios in the forecasting period, including the effects of changes in tax rates, schedules, exemptions, tax administration, and tax avoidance.

1/ In practice, in the framework of the design of Fund supported stabilization and adjustment programs, such tax estimates will generally be required for the preparation of alternative revenue projections, e.g., for an assessment of official forecasts or alternative specifications of the fiscal policy stance. Original revenue projections would usually be elaborated by the fiscal authorities based on detailed information on tax bases and the parameters of individual tax categories.

Box 2

b. Nontax revenue

Nontax revenue usually includes receipts from property income, fees and charges, non-industrial sales, the operating surplus of departmental enterprises, fines, forfeits, and private donations. Systematic relationships may be found for certain components of nontax revenue, but many items often exhibit substantial volatility. Consequently, projections of nontax revenue are often made on the basis of judgement, or simple ad hoc procedures. Sometimes forecasts are prepared for total nontax revenue by applying last year's ratio of nontax revenue to GDP to the projected value of GDP. However, rather than relying on a mechanistic projection of the aggregate, it might be feasible to allow for expected changes in relevant factors through judgmental adjustments in individual components.

c. Expenditure

Unlike government revenues, there is much less scope for forecasting the level of government expenditures through reliance on causal economic relations. This follows from the essentially political nature of the process through which decisions on public expenditure are made, which means that changes in government expenditure are in large part discretionary. Consideration may, however, be given to endogenous determination of some of the major categories within an economic classification of expenditure. Interest payments will reflect interest rates and the size of the government debt while transfers may be related to the level of economic activity. Wages and salaries are likely to be affected by government incomes policy, as well as prices and pressure in the labor market. Budget estimates are usually available, indicating the authorities' own expectations for major expenditure categories. Analysis of past relations between estimates and outcomes may indicate errors in such estimates.

d.   Financing of the budget balance

Forecasts of financing focus on three primary items: external financing; domestic nonbank borrowing; and domestic borrowing from the banking system.

Regarding external financing projections, the foreign borrowing plans and amortization schedules of finance ministries should be cross-checked with foreign lending projections and amortization schedules of lending agencies. If the level or structure of foreign debt is a problem, the projections should be cast against a broader exercise specifically addressed to the issue of external debt management. Budgetary projections for external finance should be consistent with official capital movements in the balance of payments.

For domestic nonbank borrowing, a forecast is required of the net amount of debt instruments the government will be able to place with domestic financial institutions and other domestic lenders. In this context, consideration should be given to the likely impact on the costs and availability of funds to finance non-government activities. Finally, if appropriate, the required net financing by the banking system is obtained as a residual and the result is checked against the original objectives with respect to monetary expansion.

2. Application to Hungary and other economies in transition

a.   Revenue forecasting

The task of projecting government revenues for the reference period in the case of Hungary raises difficulties that are likely to arise also in other economies in transition toward a market economy, for three main reasons:

(1)   For most tax categories, functional relationships between revenue outturns and proxy tax bases for the period of central planning may have to be viewed with great prudence. Formal relationships that may be estimated may conceal more a

pattern of nonparametric tax regimes or parametric taxes subject to frequent and haphazard changes, than a stable behavioral and institutional environment on which reliable tax functions should be predicated.

(2)   The tax regimes applied during the period of central planning were so different from the tax systems that are being introduced in the period of transition that the latter reforms amount to a replacement of virtually all former tax categories by new taxes more typical for market economies. As a consequence, even reasonably stable historical relationships between tax revenues and proxy tax bases that might be obtained for the period of central planning may provide little guidance for the projection of revenues in the transition period.

(3)   Even in the possible absence of deliberate fiscal policy measures, structural reforms introduced in other areas of the economy may have significant repercussions on the revenue outturn during the transition period by affecting the revenue base or the parameters defining the structure of the tax system.

(1)   Taxes on international trade

A review of the development of the tax system in Hungary suggests that the estimation of a functional relationship between revenues and proxy tax bases for forecasting purposes may be worthwhile only in the case of import duties. Since adequate information is not available on the record and the effects of discretionary adjustments of import tariffs, the functions will be specified for the relationship between actual import duties collected (TM) and the proxy tax base represented by total merchandise imports (c.i.f.) from the nonruble area (NRM). 1/ The parameters of the equations are estimated by the technique of ordinary least squares. Given the limited number of observations, the regression estimates have to be evaluated with caution. The equations are shown in Box 3 with t ratios in parenthesis.

The other major tax that was primarily levied on international trade transactions—the producers' differential turnover tax—was nonparametric and was mainly a function of the volume and composition of ruble imports and the ruble import prices negotiated in bilateral trade agreements with CMEA partners, the exchange rate of the forint vis-à-vis the ruble, and the domestic prices of the traded products. Given that these factors are subject to discretionary government decisions or the outcome of annual official trade negotiations, it would be difficult to project revenue from the producers' differential turnover tax without access to adequate background information from official sources. Moreover, revenue from this tax—which amounted to about 4 percent of GDP and 8 percent of total tax revenue in 1989—was highly dependent on the progress of price and trade reforms in Hungary and other CMEA countries; virtually the entire revenue of the tax would be lost as a consequence of a transition to using world market prices in trade among CMEA members.

1/ Expressed in billions of forint (Ft). Nonruble imports in Ft terms are obtained by converting nonruble imports in U.S. dollar terms at the annual average Ft/US$ exchange rate.

```
┌─────────────────────────────────────────────────────────────────┐
│                                                                   │
│                Regression Equation for Import Duties              │
│                        Period: 1982-89                            │
│                                                                   │
│                                                                   │
│                                                                   │
│              TM_t = -7.464 + 0.169 * NRM_t                        │
│                    (1.92)   (10.24)                               │
│                                                                   │
│                                                                   │
│         R̄² = 0.94                    D.W. = 1.72                  │
│                                                                   │
│                                                                   │
│                                                                   │
│              Ln TM_t = -2.920 + 1.169 Ln NRM_t                    │
│                        (4.08)     (8.86)                          │
│                                                                   │
│                                                                   │
│         R̄² = 0.91                    D.W. = 1.59                  │
│                                                                   │
│    where:                                                         │
│                                                                   │
│         TM  =  actual import duties collected.                    │
│         NRM =  total merchandise imports (c.i.f.) from the        │
│                nonruble area, expressed in billions of forint.    │
│                                                                   │
└─────────────────────────────────────────────────────────────────┘
```

Box 3

(2) Income, payroll, and turnover taxes

In the absence of tax functions and adequate microeconomic information on tax bases and structural parameters of the new taxes, revenue projections can be based on information on tax buoyancies or revenue ratios to proxy tax bases that can be derived from data observed since the inception of the tax reform. However, buoyancy cannot be measured for the EPT—which was introduced only in 1989. Furthermore, buoyancies are difficult to adjust appropriately for the effects of nonrecurrent changes in the structure of the GTT and PIT as well as in the progress of addressing the initial inadequacies of tax administration and of containing tax evasion between the first and the second year of the introduction of the new taxes. Therefore, *ratios of revenues to proxy tax bases in the year preceding the reference period are proposed as a guidance for revenue projections.*

Some available information on the relationship of potential proxy tax bases to aggregates that will be projected in other parts of the financial programming exercise and on parameters describing the structure of the taxes in 1989 is provided in Tables 4-7. The material is intended to facilitate the task of selecting appropriate proxy tax bases and incorporating assumptions concerning the specification of fiscal policy in the reference period into the tax revenue forecasting exercise.

161

(3) Other taxes

For the projection of the remaining taxes—property taxes of the local authorities, other taxes on goods and services, and miscellaneous other taxes—it is quite difficult to obtain information on plausible proxy tax bases. It may be appropriate, therefore, to project these tax revenues in the reference year on the basis of their historical ratios to GDP.

Table 4. Hungary: Household Income and the PIT

	1989 Billions of Forint	1989 Percent of GDP
(1) Gross household disposable income	1,116.7	64.5
(2) Plus: Total taxes paid	147.2	8.5
(3) Gross household income 1 + 2	1,263.9	73.0
(4) Less: Nontaxable income 1/	657.3	38.0
(5) Taxable income 3 − 4	606.6	35.1
(Percent of gross household income; 5/3)	(48.0)	(...)
(5a) Interest and dividends 2/	48.0	2.8
(5b) Income subject to progressive tax	558.6	32.3
(6) Income tax paid 7 + 8	94.2	5.4
(Percent of gross household income; 6/3)	(7.5)	(...)
(Percent of taxable income; 6/5)	(15.5)	(...)
(7) Tax on interest and dividends	9.6	0.6
(Percent of taxable income; 7/5)	(1.5)	(...)
(8) Progressive tax	84.6	4.9
(Percent of taxable income; 8/5)	(14.0)	(...)
(9) GDP at market prices	1,730.4	100.0

Sources: Central Statistical Office; Ministry of Finance; and Fund staff estimates.

1/ Fringe benefits, social benefits, and other deductions and allowances.
2/ Subject to a final 20 percent withholding tax.

Table 5. Hungary: Enterprise Profits and Profit Taxation

		1989	
		Billions of Forint	Percent of GDP
(1)	Profits before taxes net of depreciation	302.5	17.5
(2)	Less: Deduction and allowances	54.5	3.1
(3)	Taxable profits 1 − 2	248.0	14.3
	(Percent of profits before taxes; 3/1)	(82.0)	(...)
(4)	Revenue from profits 1/	120.2	6.9
	(Percent of profits before taxes; 4/1)	(39.7)	(...)
	(Percent of taxable profits; 4/3)	48.5	(...)
(5)	Less: Profit transfers from enterprises	17.2	1.0
	(Percent of taxable profits; 5/3)	(6.9)	(...)
(6)	Revenue from EPT 4 − 5 = 7 + 8	103.0	6.0
	(Percent of taxable profits; 6/3)	(41.5)	(...)
(7)	Less: Estimated once-and-for-all 1989 4 percent surtax on profits	9.9	0.6
(8)	Revenue from EPT excluding surtax 6-7	93.1	5.4
	(Percent of taxable profits; 8/3)	(37.5)	(...)
(9)	GDP at market prices	1,730.4	100.0

Sources: Central Statistical Office; Ministry of Finance; and Fund staff estimates.

1/ Including profit transfers to the budget from government owned financial and nonfinancial enterprises.

Table 6. Hungary: Household Income and Social Security Contributions

	1989	
	Billions of Forint	Percent of GDP
(1) Gross household income	1,263.9	73.0
(2) Less: Benefits and nonlabor income	520.7	30.0
(3) Gross labor income in cash 1/ 1 − 2	743.2	43.0
(Percent of gross household income)	(58.8)	(...)
(4) Less: General government wages and salaries	141.6	8.2
(5) Gross labor income in cash from non-government activities 1/ 3 − 4	601.6	34.8
(Percent of gross household income; 5/1)	(47.6)	(...)
(6) Total social security contributions	292.3	16.9
(Percent of labor income in cash; 6/3)	(39.3)	(...)
(7) Less: Employer's contributions of government institutions and local authorities	48.4	2.8
(Percent of government salaries; 7/4)	(34.2)	(...)
(8) Contributions in general Government accounts 2/ 6 − 7	243.9	14.1
(Percent of labor income from non-government activities; 8/5)	(40.5)	(...)
(9) GDP at market prices	1,730.4	100.0

Sources: Central Statistical Office; Ministry of Finance; and Fund staff estimates.

1/ Includes income from self employment.
2/ Excluding contributions from within the government sector.

Table 7. Hungary: Private Consumption and Turnover Taxes

	1989	
	Billions of Forint	Percent of GDP
(1) Consumer expenditure		
Standard SNA definition	1,059.8	61.2
Less: Net foreign tourism 1/	9.4	0.5
Official definition 2/	1,050.4	60.7
(2) Turnover tax and excise revenue (3) + (4)	230.7	13.3
(Percent of official consumer expenditure)	(22.0)	(...)
(3) GTT revenue	135.1	7.8
(Percent of official consumer expenditure)	(12.9)	(...)
(4) Excise revenue	95.6	5.5
(Percent of official consumer expenditure)	(9.1)	(...)
(5) GDP at market prices	1,730.4	100.0
Memorandum item		
Revenue loss due to widening of GTT rebate on investment goods 3/	23.0	1.3

Sources: Central Statistical Office; Ministry of Finance; and Fund staff estimates.

1/ Exempt from turnover taxes.
2/ Consumer expenditures by residents and nonresidents in Hungary.
3/ The GTT rebate on investment goods was scheduled to be introduced in annual steps of 20 percent during 1988-92.

(4) Nontax revenue

The usual difficulties in forecasting nontax revenue are exacerbated in the case of Hungary by inaccuracies of the historical data that stem from a poor monitoring of the transactions of central budgetary institutions. Data limitations have interfered with a satisfactory consolidation of these transactions in the central government accounts and may have contributed to the large fluctuations of the series over time. As a result, official projections of nontax revenue have also exhibited considerable forecasting errors.

b. Expenditure forecasting

The difficulties that generally arise in forecasting government outlays are intensified in Hungary and other transition economies by the significant expenditure effects of ongoing systemic reforms. As a consequence, forecasts of government expenditures will be subject to a particularly large degree of uncertainty.

(1) Expenditures on goods and services

Government wages and other operating expenditures are likely to be influenced in a transition economy by institutional reforms aimed at replacing government institutions that had been involved in the direct control of the economy by a government administration that enforces new procedures to underpin the efficient operation of a market economy. Given the numerous indispensable new tasks that government did not address under central planning, while it maintained a highly pervasive but meanwhile redundant presence in the economy and society otherwise, it is difficult to assess a priori the net effect of these reforms on current government outlays. Nominal current expenditures are liable to rise, however, as a consequence of tax, wage, and price reforms. Forecasts have to take into account the effects of wage increases through grossing up when an income tax is introduced and wage controls are relaxed and of price rises that are likely to be associated with a lifting of administrative controls and the adoption of a modern turnover tax system.

(2) Interest payments

Most of the outstanding government debt of Hungary is owed to the central bank or the USSR at fixed nonmarket interest rates. Such rates may be adjusted retroactively, e.g., in the context of banking and financial market reforms. Thus, adequate information on the servicing of outstanding government debt can only be obtained from official sources.

Interest payments on new debt depend on more flexible market oriented interest rates and new borrowing. The iterative process involved in the projection of such interest payments should be noted, as, ceteris paribus, they influence the size of the government deficit which determines the level of new debt that underlies the interest payments.

(3) Subsidies and transfers

In a market economy, subsidy and transfer payments may represent expenditure categories that can plausibly be considered to be endogenously determined, based on established schemes and facilities. It follows from the earlier discussion of the specific role of these expenditures in centrally planned economies, that a marked reduction of the scope of such outlays is a key objective of the restructuring of government and redefinition of the role of the budget during the transition to a market economy. The pace of the moderation of such expenditures depends on the progress of other reforms—notably price reform, the restructuring and privatization of state enterprises, and social security reform. Moveover, as illustrated by Hungary's experience in 1989, partial setbacks may be encountered as support schemes carried out through quasi-fiscal operations outside the government sector in the period of central planning are brought under the purview of the budget, resulting in a partial temporary relapse of transfer payments. The projection of subsidy and transfer payments is, therefore, contingent on adequate information concerning important elements of the Government's structural reform program, and highly sensitive to the authorities' attitude toward the pace and consistent implementation of the reforms.

(4) Capital expenditure

Compared with current expenditures, capital outlays appear to be less predetermined by other important actions associated with the transition to a market economy. A likely decline in capital transfers to a shrinking state enterprise sector may also lend greater flexibility to the projection of capital spending. However, forecasts will have to take account of compelling needs to remedy the neglect of important areas of the infrastructure under socialist central planning. This places limits on the reduction of capital outlays that should not be exceeded lest the restoration of the growth potential of the economy would be jeopardized.

c. Financing of the budget balance

A specific concern regarding forecasts of the financing of the budget balance in a transition economy is related to the typical weakness of capital markets that limits the scope of domestic nonmonetary financing. Forecasters will need to take stock of the financial instruments at the disposal of the authorities in a particular phase of the transition and assess the availability of potential captive financial resources that may be directed by the authorities to investment in government securities.

Exercises and Issues for Discussion

1. Exercises

a. Forecast total general government revenue for 1990 in the format used in Table 8. In preparing the forecast, draw on the following background information:

 • The forecast of nominal GDP at market prices from the output and price projections;

 • The forecast of the value of nonruble imports from the foreign trade/balance of payments projections;

 • The following ratios derived from *official* macroeconomic forecasts for 1990:

	Percent
Gross household income/GDP	74.0
Profits before taxes net of depreciation/GDP	17.7
Gross labor income in cash/gross household income	58.4
Official definition of consumer expenditure/GDP	61.0
Producers' differential turnover tax/GDP	3.6
Nontax revenue/GDP	7.9

b. Calculate revenue buoyancies for the main tax categories.

c. Prepare a forecast of the overall general government balance in 1990 using the format of Table 9. The option is provided to draw on the following information for 1990, recognizing that deviations from projections have regularly occurred in the past and that the figures need to be consistent with the overall macroeconomic scenario.

	Billions of forint
Projected government outlays on:	
Wages and salaries	152.9
Other goods and services	270.0
Interest payments	60.5
Subsidies and transfers	628.0
Fixed capital formation	85.0
Capital transfers	6.7
Projected GDP at market prices	2,026.0

d.   Provide an assessment of the likely resort of the Government to external and domestic nonmonetary financing of the budget balance. The former should be consistent with the projections of capital flows incorporated in the balance of payments workshop. Derive bank financing as a residual. The net repayment of nonconvertible currency debt by the Government in 1990 was officially planned at Ft. 8.6 billion.

2. Issues for discussion

a.   Review the likely effect of the following factors on the development of the main components of revenues and expenditures in 1990, commenting on the risks they represent for the realization of the revenue and outlay projections:

- Fall in real domestic output;
- Accelerating inflation;
- Pickup of consumer expenditures;
- Growth of nonruble imports;
- Depreciation of the exchange rate;
- Decline of ruble imports;
- Price and wage reform in Hungary; and
- Restructuring and privatization of state enterprises.

b.   Discuss the way the tax buoyancies in 1989 are likely to deviate from underlying tax elasticities for the same tax categories and how the buoyancies are likely to change in 1990.

c.   Comment on the considerations that determine if the forecast government accounts are consistent with the overall macroeconomic projections.

d.   Comment on changes in the structure of revenues and expenditures that appear desirable in the medium term.

Table 8. Hungary: General Government Tax Revenue

(In billions of forint)

	1982	1983	1984	1985	1986	1987	1988	1989	1990 Reference	Program
Income taxes	106.5	125.4	132.4	108.8	129.6	155.4	184.9	214.4		
Individuals	4.3	8.0	8.7	9.6	8.4	9.5	66.3	94.2		
Enterprises	102.2	117.4	123.7	99.2	121.2	145.9	118.6	120.2		
Payroll taxes	75.7	81.6	114.4	162.2	180.9	190.4	203.2	243.9		
Social security contributions	74.5	81.6	114.4	134.3	141.3	147.8	188.9	243.9		
Taxes on wages and earnings	1.2	0.0	0.0	27.9	39.6	42.6	14.3	0.0		
Property taxes	22.5	30.6	38.8	28.3	23.2	25.2	7.0	6.2		
Net wealth, corporate	13.5	13.0	13.5	19.4	17.5	19.8	--	--		
Confiscation and other	0.4	8.8	17.4	0.2	0.3	--	0.8	--		
Local property taxes	8.6	8.8	7.9	8.7	5.4	5.4	6.2	6.2		
Taxes on goods and services	208.8	223.1	209.1	204.8	220.0	241.9	361.4	369.3		
Consumer turnover taxes and excises	72.5	83.6	88.0	94.0	105.5	127.5	211.8	230.7		
Producers' differential turnover taxes	94.1	94.9	72.7	73.1	57.3	60.6	93.9	65.9		
Import duties	23.1	24.8	24.5	27.6	32.7	34.7	36.3	48.9		
Other taxes on goods and services	19.1	19.8	23.9	10.1	24.5	19.1	19.4	23.8		
Other taxes	7.1	13.6	19.9	11.8	15.0	30.1	4.4	2.2		
Total tax revenue	420.6	474.3	514.6	515.9	568.7	643.0	760.9	836.0		

Source: IMF Institute data base.

Table 9. Hungary: Operations of the General Government

(In billions of forint)

	1982	1983	1984	1985	1986	1987	1988	1989	1990 Reference Progr
Revenue	501.6	545.6	594.8	620.1	669.4	724.8	892.9	1,019.0	
Tax Revenue 1/	420.6	474.3	514.6	515.9	568.7	642.9	760.9	836.0	
Nontax revenue 2/	81.0	71.3	80.2	104.2	100.7	81.9	132.0	183.0	
Total expenditure 3/	519.2	555.1	581.2	631.9	703.5	768.4	892.3	1,041.5	
Current expenditure	440.2	479.9	503.8	550.2	616.0	669.1	783.2	929.3	
Wages and salaries	63.2	65.5	70.4	81.1	87.8	92.9	122.9	141.6	
Other goods and services	99.1	94.6	103.2	112.7	123.8	146.8	179.6	208.6	
Interest payments	9.4	2.1	5.5	3.7	14.1	31.6	22.5	41.3	
Subsidies and transfers	268.5	317.7	324.7	352.7	390.3	397.8	458.2	537.8	
Capital expenditure 3/	79.0	75.2	77.4	81.7	87.5	99.2	109.1	112.2	
Fixed capital formation	50.9	68.9	71.0	71.8	70.4	73.2	88.6	101.2	
Capital transfers 3/	28.1	6.3	6.4	9.9	17.1	26.0	20.5	11.0	
Overall balance	-17.6	-9.5	13.6	-11.8	-34.1	-43.5	0.6	-22.6	
Financing	17.6	9.5	-13.6	11.8	34.1	43.5	-0.6	22.6	
External financing	2.9	4.1	1.3	-1.1	-2.8	-7.7	-8.4	-10.3	
Domestic financing	14.7	5.4	-14.9	12.9	36.9	51.2	7.8	32.9	
Bank borrowing, net	...	4.2	-10.8	2.9	58.4	50.3	7.5	55.0	
Nonbank borrowing	...	1.2	-4.1	10.0	-21.5	0.9	0.3	-22.1	

Source: IMF Institute database.

1/ Including profit transfers from government-owned financial and nonfinancial enterprises.
2/ Including capital revenue.
3/ Including a small amount of lending less repayments.

VII. Monetary Sector

Institutional and Recent Monetary Developments in Hungary

1. Institutional developments

a. Establishment of a two-tier banking system

Before 1987 the banking system was essentially of the *monobank* variety, characteristic of centrally planned economies. The dominant financial institution, the National Bank of Hungary (NBH), was both the central bank and the prime commercial bank for the enterprise sector. Banking services to households were provided separately by the National Savings Bank and a network of saving cooperatives. In addition, the financial system included several small joint venture banks and a limited number of specialized financial institutions, such as the Foreign Trade Bank—which was mainly involved in the financing of external trade—and the State Development Bank—which largely operated with budgetary funds to finance state initiated investments.

This system was substantially changed on January 1, 1987. A *two-tier banking* system was established with the separation of the central and commercial banking functions of the NBH. Commercial bank operations of the NBH and the State Development Bank were taken over by three newly created commercial banks. Two previously existing specialized banking institutions, including the Foreign Trade Bank, also received commercial bank charters. These five banks formed the core of the banking system dealing with enterprises. In the course of 1987, the requirement for enterprises to keep their current accounts with a particular commercial bank was lifted and administrative regulations on interest rates on enterprise deposits and loans were abolished.

The segmentation between banking services for enterprises and the traditional network of savings institutions for households was, however, preserved. This left financial institutions for households practically untouched in this first phase of banking reform.

b. Integration of household and enterprise banking

A first step in integrating enterprise and household banking was taken in 1988. Commercial banks were allowed to issue certificates of deposit to households at competitive interest rates but continued to be prevented from accepting other forms of deposit. By end 1989, the stock of certificates of deposits, although still small in absolute terms, had reached about 4 percent of household's deposits.

The necessary steps for fuller integration, however, were not taken until 1989. Until then, household deposit rates had been administratively set at very low levels to finance the subsidization of housing loans. These loans were the main type of credit extended to households by the National Savings Bank and were supplied at extremely low interest rates (0–3 percent). Under this system there was thus considerable cross-subsidization from household depositors to household borrowers. These arrangements needed to be changed before the household banking system could be put on a competitive basis. In 1989, interest rates on housing loans were raised and the remaining subsidy on new housing loans was assumed by the budget. Moreover, the existing stock of low interest housing loans was transferred to a newly established housing fund in exchange for bonds with market-related yields. While interest rate ceilings on household deposits remained, they were increasingly adjusted in line with movements in market rates (Table 1).

c. Toward a more competitive banking system

The number of financial institutions grew rapidly in response to the initiatives described above. For example, by end 1989 the number of commercial banks had reached 20, 13 of which were Hungarian owned. 1/ Despite the expansion in the number of financial institutions, activity remained very concentrated and the process of integrating household and enterprise business was slow. The three new commercial banks that inherited the portfolio of the NBH, together with the National Savings Bank, accounted for over 85 percent of the deposit base and a similar share of total assets. 2/ As discussed below and in the following sections, a number of other factors slowed the pace of change. These included the inherited fragile credit portfolios of the major commercial banks, the strong dependence of commercial banks on central bank refinancing, a thin capital market, and some features of the regulatory environment.

Despite the measures taken to integrate enterprise and household banking, the National Savings Bank and savings cooperatives continued to account for the bulk of household operations. While rapid transformation was not to be expected, the regulatory environment may also have had an effect. Notably, high reserve requirements were imposed on deposits of households at commercial banks in order to protect the savings cooperatives from a rapid drain of funds.

Although the newly incorporated commercial banks were profitable in their first three years of operation, the quality of their asset portfolios remained poor. Credits continued to be largely extended to the enterprises that accounted for the largest share of the pre-reform portfolio. This in part reflected the lack of incentives and regulatory requirements for banks to recognize losses resulting from bad loans in their portfolios. In addition, the Bankruptcy Law, enacted in 1986, while used to liquidate small enterprises on a modest scale, had little or no effect on large state enterprises. Unchanged, if not worsening, portfolio composition probably also reflected the small number of both large borrowers and banks, which inevitably resulted in strong links between them.

1/ The remainder of the banking system consisted of four specialized banking institutions, including the National Savings Bank, 9 specialized financial institutions, 5 insurance companies, and 262 savings cooperatives.

2/ Natinal Bank of Hungary, Annual Report 1990, p. 45.

Table 1. Hungary: Selected Interest Rates

	1987	1988	1989	
			(Percent per annum at end-year)	
I. Deposits			Gross 2/	Net 2/
Households 1/				
Sight	2.0	2.0	8.0	8.0
Current account	5.0	7.0	12.0	12.0
Time, fixed for				
One year	9.0	13.5	16.9	13.5
Two years	10.0	14.0	17.5	14.0
Three years	12.5	15.0	18.8	15.0
Housing, fixed for				
Less than five years	8.0	14.0	14.0	14.0
More than five years	11.0	18.0	18.0	18.0
Securities				
Savings notes (fixed for six years)	13.5	16.5	20.6	16.5
Certificates of deposits	...	18.0	21.0	16.8
Enterprises 3/				
Current account (maximum)	...	15.5	13.0	...
Maturity				
Less than 1 month	...	11.9	17.5	...
Less than 1 year	3-9	14.2	19.0	...
More than 1 year	11-12	15.6	20.6	...
II. Credits			Rate	Fee
Households 4/				
Housing loans	0-3	0-3	18.5	1.0
Nonpreferential housing	8.0	12.0	20.0	2.0
Hire purchase loans	12.0	13.0	20.0	4.0
Personal loans	13.2	15.2	20.0	4.0
Enterprises 3/				
Maturity				
Less than 1 year	13.0	18.3	23.0	...
More than 1 year	12.0	16.9	20.3	...
Discounted bills of exchange	11.5	14.9	19.1	...
Interbank market	...	...	27.9	...
National Bank of Hungary				
State loans	10.0	11.5	11.5	...
Refinancing credits				
Overdraft facility	11.5	13.0	17.0	...
Liquidity loans	...	...	21.0	...
Over one-year maturity (basic rate)	10.5	14.0	17.0	...
Rediscount of commercial bills of exchange 1/	9.5	10.5-13.5	14.0-17.0	...

Source: IMF Institute data base.

1/ In 1989 the distribution of deposits was: 6 percent sight and current accounts; 79 percent time deposits; 7 percent housing deposits; and 8 percent foreign currency deposits.

2/ In 1989, a 20 percent withholding tax was introduced on interest payments to households.

3/ Data for 1988-89 are averages; for 1987, they are in terms of ranges.

4/ The bulk of loans to households are for housing.

One consequence of these circumstances was that the burden of a tightening of monetary policy was born disproportionately by viable enterprises which tended to be crowded out of the credit market because of continuing credit expansion to nonperforming enterprises.

d. Policy instruments

The general direction of change was to increase reliance on indirect instruments of monetary control. The principal instrument of monetary control, however, was central bank refinancing quotas, including rediscounting of commercial bills. By varying the volume of credit extended to commercial banks, the NBH was able to exert considerable influence over the amount of resources available to banks for their lending operations.

In 1989 central bank refinancing credits accounted for nearly one third of banking system credit to enterprises and households; nearly three-quarters of long-term bank lending was covered by refinancing credits. These were a cheaper form of financing than deposits because they were subject only to a liquid asset requirement, and not a reserve requirement as were deposits. Bank specific refinancing credit ceilings were linked to a bank's equity and capital. On this basis, they were adjusted whenever the overall quota for central bank refinancing credits was revised.

The introduction of an auction market in Treasury bills in December 1988 facilitated use of a more flexible interest rate policy. These bills were well received due to their liquidity and competitive rates (26.5-27 percent at end 1989). However, with only a small amount of bills issued, the scope for open market operations remained limited. Reflecting the methods of credit allocation by the NBH, the authorities' main instrument for influencing interest rates continued to be the terms on which, through various "windows", they provided refinancing to the commercial banks. While changes in rates on refinancing credits from the NBH had been small in 1987-88, there were larger increases in 1989 (see Table 1). At the end of 1989 the basic refinancing rate used for longer-term credits stood at 17 percent while the more widely used liquidity rate for working capital needs was 21 percent (compared to an inflation rate of 17 percent).

A system of reserve requirements, introduced in early 1987, served largely prudential purposes. A uniform rate was introduced for reserve requirements in 1989 (which was raised from 15 percent to 18 percent in September 1989), 1/ although these requirements did not apply to all liabilities, with external liabilities and refinancing credits excluded. Interest payments on reserve deposits were discontinued in 1989.

Interbank lending continued to be intermediated by NBH and turnover remained low.

1/ The National Saving Bank continued to have distinct reserve requirements from commercial banks.

e.   Foreign exchange transactions

An important step in expanding the scope of banking operations was the relaxation of restrictions on foreign exchange transactions. In 1988, commercial banks were authorized to provide foreign exchange-related services, including the provision of special travel accounts in foreign exchange. 1/ From September 1989, banks were effectively free to collect all forms of deposits in foreign exchange of households. They were also permitted to extend foreign currency loans to Hungarian enterprises and households, at their own risk. Trade related foreign exchange operations remained prohibited.

f.   Other financial assets

The bond and securities markets were too small to create strong competition for commercial banks. The thinness of these markets also forestalled significant financial flows between households and enterprises that could otherwise have mitigated the effects of the separation of household and enterprise banks. The relative attractiveness of bonds waned after the authorities ceased issuing government guarantees for bonds issued to households in early 1987; bonds also became less attractive as the main underwriters refrained from adjusting bond prices, despite the rapid rise in interest rates and increasing competition from treasury bills and certificates of deposits. The most notable development in the capital markets was the increase in the volume of shares sold by enterprises, from FT 48 billion in 1988 to FT 150 billion in 1989.

2. Monetary developments in 1989

Monetary developments in 1989 were dominated by the weakness of the fiscal position and the large unplanned external payments surplus in nonconvertible currencies. Both these factors contributed to high bank liquidity, which downward adjustments to the NBH refinancing limits were insufficient to offset. As a result, credit to the state enterprise sector grew by 21.5 percent, compared with a slight decline in 1988. Household credits grew by considerably less (5.5 percent) reflecting the increased costs of housing loans. These developments, together with the financing needs of the fiscal sector, resulted in total domestic credit of the banking system increasing by about 22 percent, or over twice the rate of 1988.

The easing of credit conditions was accompanied by a much larger than planned increase of private consumption. Enterprises, which enjoyed greater freedom over wage determination following a liberalization of the wage system in January 1989, granted large wage increases and social benefits continued to grow rapidly. The wage bill of socialized enterprises is estimated to have risen by 19 percent, compared to a planned increase of 6-7 percent. Another important factor

---

1/ Residents were allowed to declare convertible currency holdings from non-specified sources without legal sanction; seventy-five percent was allowed to be deposited in a special travel account.

contributing to the growth of private consumption was the accelerated spending abroad, reflecting the liberalization of regulations on personal imports and travel abroad in 1988. This increase in spending underlay a further small rise in inflation and a sharp deterioration of the external current balance in convertible currencies.

The strong growth in credit was partly reflected in a faster rate of growth of broad money (12 percent in 1989 compared with 2 percent in 1988). This increase in liquidity was held by enterprises whose deposits grew by 26 percent, which was more than the growth of GDP. By contrast, household deposits actually declined in nominal terms, reflecting the noted drawdown of travel allowances (whether for travel, private imports, or holdings of foreign currency) as well as a significant prepayment of housing loans to avoid an anticipated new tax on the interest payments of these loans (this tax was later deemed unconstitutional). Note, however, that currency in circulation, most of which was held by households, increased substantially (10 percent). The increased relative importance of currency in household's financial portfolios is consistent with their observed increase in real spending.

Compounding the problems of excess liquidity in the economy was a loosening of financial discipline in the enterprise sector, as reflected by a significant increase in the stock of forced inter-enterprise credits, i.e., a build-up of inter-enterprise arrears. These arrears are estimated to have reached FT 127 billion, equivalent to 7.5 percent of GDP or about half of the short-term credit extended by banks to enterprises (certain estimates put the total as high as FT 200 billion). 1/ This debt was believed to stem from a relatively small number of enterprises (30–40) whose insolvency placed about 400 other enterprises in financial difficulty. These arrears, which were in effect a substitute for bank credit, complicated the task of managing the liquidity of the economy.

1/ National Bank of Hungary, 1989 Annual Report, p. 10.

Forecasting the Monetary Survey

1. Introduction

The liabilities of the banking system to the private sector and state enterprises (currency, demand deposits, time and savings deposits) are called *monetary aggregates*. These aggregates have been found to play an important role in the determination of real output, prices, and the balance of payments, which indicate some of the final objectives of economic policy. The forecasting of monetary aggregates is thus a crucial step in the design of monetary policy.

In formulating monetary policy, the authorities must ultimately have in mind the relationship between the monetary instruments under their control and their final objectives. However, these relationships are typically indirect and can be thought of as having two components: (1) the link between monetary aggregates that represent *intermediate targets* and *final objectives*; and (2) that between *policy instruments* and *intermediate targets*.

The *monetary survey* provides a framework for analyzing the desired values for the variables for which the authorities can set intermediate targets, i.e., monetary aggregates. It reflects the consolidation of the balance sheets of the different components of the banking system, i.e., the sum of transactions of the NBH and commercial banks, netting out all inter-bank transactions. Monetary aggregates represent the counterpart of, and by definition must be equal to, the sum of net foreign assets (valued in local currency) and net domestic credit (including other items, net) (Box 1).

Stylized Monetary Survey

Assets	Liabilities
Net Foreign Assets	Monetary Aggregates
Credit	Broad money
To government (net)	Currency in circulation
To households	Demand deposits
To enterprises	Time and savings deposits
To other	
	Other (less liquid) financial
Other items (net)	assets

Box 1

The link between policy instruments and intermediate targets is discussed below in the context of the balance sheet of the monetary authorities.

2. Determinants of monetary aggregates and forecasting tecniques

a. Demand for and supply of monetary aggregates

For analytical and forecasting purposes, a key distinction must be drawn between monetary aggregates defined in *real terms* (at constant prices) and in *nominal terms* (at current prices).

Money is voluntarily held to finance a flow of transactions and as a savings asset. The amount of money willingly held by the general public will be assessed in terms of its real value, i.e., the purchasing power of money over a representative basket of goods. For instance, if prices all doubled and then stayed at their new level, the public would need to hold exactly twice as much money on average as it would otherwise to conduct any given amount of real transactions. While the demand for money should, thus, be thought of in real terms, the monetary authorities can only affect the nominal money stock (see section below for a discussion of the money supply process).

The impact of changes in the nominal money stock depends crucially on how movements in actual money balances, defined in real terms, compare with the demand for these real balances by the public. If the monetary authorities supply more (less) than the public wishes to hold, the public will reduce (increase) the value of this supply.

How does the public affect real money balances? There are two principal mechanisms:

(1) The public may buy (sell) foreign currency in exchange for local currency in conjunction with balance of payments transactions, i.e., imports (exports) of goods and services or capital transactions. The stock of net local currency would be reduced (increased) by the transaction, as would be the stock of foreign assets held by the monetary authorities.

(2) The public may buy (sell) domestic goods in exchange for local currency. If the public feels it has too much money as compared with real goods, purchases will increase. This increase in the demand for goods will raise domestic prices. The public will have, in effect, reduced its stock of real money balances via inflation, although the nominal stock may remain the same.

Both mechanisms may operate at the same time. If the monetary authorities supply too much (little) money, prices of local goods may increase (decrease) and the balance of payments may worsen (improve). The impact on the balance of payments will be larger the more open are the goods and capital markets and the less flexible is the exchange rate system.

For instance, in an economy with a fixed exchange rate and no exchange and trade controls, the authorities would have little control over the nominal money stock. Any imbalance between the supply of and demand for money would result in a monetary expansion or contraction through the balance of payments, with limited impact on prices. By contrast, in an economy with a fully flexible exchange rate and no controls, the exchange rate would equilibrate the supply of and demand for foreign exchange so that net foreign assets would remain unchanged. In this case, a monetary expansion would permanently increase the nominal level of monetary aggregates, the counterpart of which is likely to be an increase in prices, including the price of foreign currency (the exchange rate).

Increased spending resulting from a monetary expansion may also raise real output, especially if there is unutilized capacity. Conversely, decreased spending may reduce output, the more so if prices are inflexible downward. Taking the first case as an example, the increase in real output, by raising the number of transactions that need to be financed, should result in an increase in the demand for money. The output effect thus serves as a third avenue for restoring equilibrium. It is generally accepted that there is normally a positive relationship between the growth of monetary aggregates and nominal output. However, considerable differences of view still remain as regards the strength of this relationship and the division of the effects of changes in the nominal money supply between prices and real output.

b. Forecasting techniques

Since households and enterprises determine the real value of the monetary aggregates, forecasting these aggregates requires consideration of the behavior of these economic agents. Two general methods are discussed. One method is based on the use of *regression techniques* to estimate a *demand for money function*. The other approach is less formal and concentrates on *trends* in the *velocity of money*. The choice of methods is generally dictated by data availability and the stability over time of institutional arrangements and behavioral relations in the case in question.

(1) The demand for money equation

This method assumes that the financial behavior of economic agents can be explained as a function of a small number of economic variables. It also assumes that the relationship between monetary aggregates willingly held and the explanatory variables is stable over time. As discussed below, there are various factors that could render this relationship unstable, limiting the usefulness of this approach.

Whether to use narrow or broad definitions of the money supply in estimation should be dictated by the empirical results. It is not possible to identify a priori the aggregate for which there is the most stable demand from the public. Generally, the larger the share of the banking system's liabilities to the nongovernment sector that is included in the definition of money, the more helpful it is in forecasting the monetary survey. However, it may be more difficult for the monetary authorities to control a broadly defined monetary aggregate.

The most commonly used demand for money function includes as explanatory variables a *transaction-related* ("scale") variable, most often real GDP, and a variable measuring the *relative attractiveness of holding money* as compared with other financial or real assets.

The choice of opportunity cost variable depends to some extent on the definition of monetary aggregate being used and on the institutional arrangements of a country. Some general representative nominal interest rate could be the most appropriate measure of opportunity cost of holding monetary assets which earn no interest. For monetary assets which earn interest, a variable measuring the interest rate differential between money and other financial assets may be more appropriate. In countries where the financial liabilities of the banking system to the private sector represent the greatest part of the latter's total financial assets, the real rate of interest has sometimes been used as a proxy for the yield on financial assets relative to real assets (the expected effect of the real interest rate on the demand for the monetary aggregate being positive). Where interest rates remain unchanged for long periods, this effect may be captured by considering the rate of inflation alone (the expected effect of inflation on real money holdings being negative).

Many empirical estimations of the demand for monetary aggregates have found the most successful formulation to be in logarithmic form, except for the opportunity cost variable. For example:

$$\ln \left(\frac{M}{P}\right)_t = a_0 + a_1 \ln\left(\frac{Y}{P}\right)_t + a_2 (\pi)_t$$

$$a_1 \geq 0; \quad a_2 \lesseqgtr 0$$

(1)

where:

M = the monetary aggregate
P = the price level
Y = GDP in nominal terms
π = the opportunity cost of holding money
a_1 = income elasticity of the demand for money
a_2 = semi-elasticity of money with respect to the opportunity cost variable (the sign depending on the definition used for π)

An important assumption underlying estimation of equation (1) is that the real demand for money balances is always equal to the actual real supply. In fact, adjustment to any disequilibrium may not be instantaneous. This could reflect factors such as costs and inconveniences of spending any excess money immediately or the time that it takes to realize that a monetary expansion has occurred and that money holdings exceed their desired levels. To take account of the lags involved in returning to equilibrium, a partial-adjustment model is often used that assumes that the adjustment in a given period corresponds to a fraction, λ, of the desired adjustment.

Then, denoting by M^D and M the desired and actual amounts of the monetary aggregate in nominal terms, respectively:

$$\ln\left(\frac{M}{P}\right)_t - \ln\left(\frac{M}{P}\right)_{t-1} = \lambda\left[\ln\left(\frac{M^D}{P}\right)_t - \ln\left(\frac{M}{P}\right)_{t-1}\right] \qquad (2)$$

where $0 \leq \lambda \leq 1$

Substituting equation (1) into equation (2) and putting $\ln\left(\frac{M}{P}\right)_{t-1}$ on the right hand of the equation:

$$\ln\left(\frac{M}{P}\right)_t = b_0 + b_1 \ln\left(\frac{Y}{P}\right)_t + b_2 (\pi)_t + b_3 \ln\left(\frac{M}{P}\right)_{t-1} \qquad (3)$$

where:

$$b_0 = \lambda a_0$$
$$b_1 = \lambda a_1$$
$$b_2 = \lambda a_2$$
$$b_3 = 1 - \lambda$$

The values of coefficients b_1, b_2, and b_3 can be estimated directly from the regression. These estimated values can be used to derive the estimated values for a_1, a_2 and λ of equations (1) and (2). [1]

Table 2 summarizes the results of estimating a demand for money function for broad money in Hungary using annual data for the 1982–89 period. [2] The dependent variable is the average stock of broad money held during the period deflated by the consumer price index. The independent variables measuring the transactions motive and opportunity cost of holding money are, respectively, GDP in constant 1986 prices and the inflation rate, as measured by the consumer price index.

[1] Note that $b_3 = 1 - \lambda$ and, therefore, $\lambda = 1 - b_3$.
[2] Note that the degrees of freedom in estimation are limited by the small number of data observations. One consequence is that statistically significant results require large values for the calculated t- and F-statistics.

Table 2. Hungary: Money Demand Estimates

Period	Explanatory variables				
	$\ln\left(\frac{Y}{P}\right)$	Π	$\ln\left(\frac{M}{P}\right)_{t-1}$	Constant	
1982-89	.11	-1.15	...	5.27	(4)
	(.17)	(2.14)		(1.24)	
	$R^2 = .70$	$\bar{R}^2 = .58$	$F_{2.5} = 5.87 > F_{.95} = 5.79$		
1982-87	.45	-.81	...	2.85	(5)
	(.80)	(.64)		(.73)	
	$R^2 = .20$	$\bar{R}^2 = -$	$F_{2.3} = .38 < F_{.95} = 9.55$		
1982-89	.54	-1.42	.98	-3.59	(6)
	(1.73)	(5.32)	(4.18)	(1.22)	
	$R^2 = .94$	$\bar{R}^2 = .90$	$F_{3.4} = 22.66 > F_{.95} = 6.59$		
1982-87	.64	-2.44	1.22	-5.65	(7)
	(1.74)	(2.28)	(2.31)	(1.27)	
	$R^2 = .78$	$\bar{R}^2 = .46$	$F_{3.2} = 2.4 < F_{.95} = 19.2$		

Notes: t-values are in parenthesis

$\ln\left(\frac{M}{P}\right)_t$ = the dependent variable, is defined as the average of end of period and beginning period stock of broad money, divided by consumer price index (1982 = 100). In log terms.

$\ln\left(\frac{M}{P}\right)_{t-1}$ = $\ln\left(\frac{M}{P}\right)_t$ lagged one period.

$\ln\left(\frac{Y}{P}\right)$ = GDP at constant 1986 prices. In log terms.

Π = Percentage change in the consumer price index.

$F_{.95}$ = Critical value to be exceeded by the calculated F statistic of the regression for the overall fit of the equation to be statistically significant at the 95 percent confidence level.

186

Equation (4) assumes that the demand for money takes the form of equation (1) of the text, i.e., assuming that the desired stock of real money holdings is equal to the supply at all times. The overall fit of the equation is of borderline significance at the 95 percent confidence level. Also, while the values of the regression coefficients are of the expected sign, the estimated coefficient for real income is close to zero, a suspect result in itself.

When regression coefficients take on implausible values, or when the fit of the equation is poor, the behavioral relationship being estimated may be unstable. In order to check for instability, the equation was run over several subperiods, including for 1982–87 (see equation 5).

Not unexpectedly, the values of the regression coefficients in equation (5) are considerably different from those of equation (4). While the income coefficient is somewhat closer to what could be expected, the fit is much poorer and statistically insignificant. These results do not reveal a stable demand for money during the period in question.

Equations (6) and (7) incorporate as an explanatory variable real money balances lagged one period to capture any temporary disequilibria in the money market, as described in equation (3) of the text. For the 1982–89 period such a specification improved the fit considerably (equation 6). Note that the implied value of λ is close to zero, which suggests, implausibly, virtually no adjustment to a disequilibrium situation. 1/ When the regression was rerun over the 1982–87 period (equation 7), the estimates once again became statistically insignificant at the 95 percent confidence level and the values of the regression coefficients changed considerably, further evidence of at least one break in the behavioral relationship around 1987.

(2)   Possible estimation problems

Stability of money demand functions is predicated on an *unchanged institutional environment*. Structural reform would be expected to change the overall behavior of economic agents, thus rendering the estimation of most behavioral relationships, including the demand for money, difficult.

Take as an example the possible effects of financial reform. An improvement in the functioning and depth of financial markets could reduce the demand for money as innovations promote economies in money holdings and new, more attractive assets become available. This effect could however be partly offset if financial reform were to make savings in the form of financial assets, including money, more attractive. The responsiveness of money demand to interest rates may also appear to increase significantly because interest rates prior to liberalization did not vary sufficiently to allow for measurement of their effects on portfolio choices.

1/ Recall that the regression coefficient should be an estimate of 1-λ where $0 \leq \lambda \leq 1$; see equation (2).

Poor regression results may also be attributable to *data problems*. The data may be affected by errors or changes in definitions and collection methods. Moreover, the data series may not be long enough: the number of needed data points increases with the number of explanatory variables. In order to avoid structural shifts, while at the same time having the necessary length of time series, it is often advisable to limit the estimation period to relatively short intervals using quarterly or monthly data. Unfortunately, such data are often either unavailable for all the needed time series or their quality is considerably inferior to annual data.

A third possible explanation for poor results may be the existence of a *liquidity overhang*. A liquidity overhang may be defined as the stock of money balances in excess of desired levels (apart from reversible short run variations). Liquidity overhangs are most often associated with countries that have significant price, trade and exchange controls, which are reflected in chronic shortages of goods. If excess liquidity were to exist over certain parts of the estimation period, the regression equation would be fitting points from both the demand and supply curves of the money market, limiting the usefulness of the results.

Determining whether an overhang exists is not an easy matter since the demand for money is unobservable. Estimation of an overhang is even more difficult and will not be dealt with here. 1/ Visible signs of frustrated spending intentions in the official market, such as queues, are neither a necessary nor sufficient condition for verifying the existence of an overhang. On the one hand, spending intentions may be so totally frustrated that queuing is not worthwhile. On the other hand, queuing may reflect *relative* price distortions—i.e., excess demand for certain products offset by growing inventories of other unwanted products—rather than *absolute* price distortions—i.e., generalized excess demand for goods.

Concerns over involuntarily held liquid balances arise because they could be activated any time, either during a period of price liberalization or by such factors as a worsening in expectations about inflation and/or the supply situation, leading to a much more rapid inflation than expected and possibly to hyperinflation. Moreover, so long as an overhang exists, the link between monetary aggregates and aggregate demand is severely weakened, limiting the effectiveness of monetary policy. Excess household liquidity is also likely to diminish incentives to work for money incomes and, more generally, to carry out transactions in the legalized monetized economy.

Methods of eliminating liquidity overhangs include currency reform, i.e., reduction of the nominal money stock; a rise in the price level, by fiat or by market forces (in principle this only needs to be a "blip" in the price level; in practice it might result in an outburst of inflation); and privatization schemes that absorb any excess balances. Avoiding a recurrence of the problem requires changes in the structure of the economy, including less controls and harder budget constraints.

1/ Studies that discuss procedures for estimating the existence of a liquidity overhang include: Cottarelli, Carlo and Mario Blejer, "Forced Savings and Repressed Inflation in the Soviet Union: Some Empirical Results," *IMF, WP/91/55*; Portes, Richard and David Winter, "Disequilibrium Estimates for Consumption Goods Markets in Centrally Planned Economies," *Review of Economic Studies*, pp. 137-149, 1980; and Portes, Richard, Richard E. Quandt and Stephen Yeo, "Test of Chronic Shortage Hypothesis: the Case of Poland," *Review of Economics and Statistics*, pp. 288-95, 1988.

While excess liquidity has not generally been considered a major problem in Hungary during the 1980s, because of a less distorted price system than in other Eastern European countries, the existence of some excess liquidity cannot be completely discounted. One indication is that black market exchange rates were 20-30 percent more depreciated than the official rate between 1982 and 1988, with the premium increasing to about 40 percent in 1988-89 (Table 3). These premiums may give some indication that excess balances of local currency were being channelled into black markets. The relative significance of this factor would depend on the size of, and access to these markets.

Table 3. Hungary: Black Market and Official Exchange Rates

	Official rate	Black market rate	Premium
	(In forint per U.S. dollar)		*(In percent)*
1982	36.6	43.4	18.6
1983	42.7	53.8	26.0
1984	48.0	60.1	25.2
1985	50.1	63.7	27.2
1986	45.8	58.4	27.5
1987	47.0	61.2	30.2
1988	50.4	71.0	40.9
1989	59.1	82.0	38.7

Sources: Pick's foreign currency report, official sources, and staff estimates.

(3) Velocity of monetary circulation

Velocity of monetary circulation, V, can be defined as the number of times the money supply, however defined, turns over in a given period to finance a certain level of economic activity. If we approximate the level of economic activity by nominal gross domestic product, velocity can be represented by the following identity:

$$V = \frac{PY}{M} = \frac{Y}{\left(\frac{M}{P}\right)} \qquad (8)$$

To interpret equation (8) behaviorally rather than simply as an identity, recall that in the absence of a liquidity overhang, real money balances, $\frac{M}{P}$, are determined by the demand for these balances. Changes in velocity thus critically reflect changes in real money demand.

For example, if the income elasticity of demand for money balances were assumed to be one, i.e., a given percentage increase in real output raises the real demand for money by an equal percentage, real income changes would have no effect on velocity. On the other hand, if increasing inflationary pressures lead to the rate of return on real assets exceeding that on financial assets, the demand for money balances, at a given income level, would be expected to fall. This would result in an increase in velocity. If an overhang were to exist, i.e., involuntarily held money balances, observed velocity would be less than desired velocity. An observed downward trend in velocity could suggest the build-up of a liquidity overhang, particularly if there was no reason to expect desired velocity to decline.

The advantage of using judgmental velocity estimates rather than regression equations to forecast real money balances is that projections are not constrained by past behavioral relationships which may either be unstable or not expected to hold in the future.

Table 4 calculates the velocity of monetary circulation for the period 1980–89. In the most recent period, 1988–89, velocity rose significantly, whereas in previous years it was remarkably stable. Excluding 1988–89, average velocity (defined in terms of average broad money) was equal to 2.23, compared with 2.75 in 1989.

A major problem in interpreting the results of Table 4 is that no distinction is made between the behavior of state enterprises and households. In contrast to market economies, private ownership of enterprises is limited, which weakens the link between corporate profits and household incomes: in a market economy, corporate profits are readily translated into household incomes though dividend payments. Similarly, controls on prices and incomes weaken the mechanisms whereby any ex ante excess liquidity in one sector gets distributed across other sectors. For instance, any excess liquidity of state enterprises may be prevented from being translated into a wage increase. The fact, noted earlier, that households and enterprises bank with quite separate institutions may further weaken the financial transmission mechanisms between the sectors. For all these reasons the calculated velocities may result from very different behavioral patterns on the part of enterprises and households and thus be a misleading series to use as a basis for forecasting velocity.

Tables 5 and 6 show separate velocity calculations for households and state enterprises.

Table 4. Hungary: Velocity of Monetary Circulation of the Economy

	Nominal GDP	Money holdings 1/		Velocity 2/	
		End of period	Period average	End of period	Period average
	(In billions of forint)				
	(1)	(2)	(3)	(1)/(2)	(1)/(3)
1980	721.0	342.1	...	2.11	...
1981	779.9	365.1	353.6	2.14	2.21
1982	847.9	397.7	381.4	2.13	2.22
1983	896.4	410.5	404.1	2.18	2.21
1984	978.5	432.3	421.4	2.26	2.32
1985	1,033.7	480.8	456.6	2.15	2.26
1986	1,088.8	524.7	502.8	2.07	2.17
1987	1,226.4	582.0	553.4	2.11	2.22
1988	1,408.8	593.7	587.9	2.37	2.40
1989	1,730.4	665.6	629.7	2.60	2.75

Source: IMF Institute data base.

1/ Defined as broad money.
2/ Calculated both in relation to end of period and period average money stocks.
3/ Defined as the sum of end of period and beginning of period money stocks, and divided by two.

The velocity of monetary circulation of households (Table 5), defined as household's disposable income divided by the sum of currency in circulation and household deposits, 1/ was on a slow declining trend through 1987, followed by significant increases in 1988 and, particularly, in 1989. As discussed in the section on recent economic developments, there was a sharp fall in the demand for money of households in 1989 reflecting drawdowns of travel allowances, following an easing of regulations in 1988, and significant prepayments of housing loans to avoid an anticipated new tax. The sharp rise in household velocities in 1989 underlines the importance of identifying the effects of changes in structural and institutional developments on economic agents' behavior.

1/ In the absence of the necessary information, it is assumed that all currency in circulation is held by households. In practice, the bulk of currency in circulation would be expected to be with the household sector.

Table 5. Hungary: Velocity of Circulation of Household Money

| | Disposable incomes | Money holdings 1/ | | Velocity 2/ | |
		End of period	Period average	End of period	Period average
		(In billions of forint)			
	(1)	(2)	(3)	(1)/(2)	(1)/(3)
1980	461.8	213.9	...	2.16	...
1981	501.2	235.0	224.5	2.13	2.23
1982	539.2	252.5	243.8	2.13	2.21
1983	581.3	280.3	266.4	2.07	2.18
1984	634.0	309.3	294.8	2.05	2.15
1985	695.2	342.1	325.7	2.03	2.13
1986	747.8	383.5	362.8	1.95	2.06
1987	814.6	415.0	399.3	1.96	2.04
1988	936.9	448.6	431.8	2.09	2.17
1989	1,116.7	453.8	451.2	2.46	2.47

Source: IMF Institute data base.

1/ Defined as the sum of currency in circulation and household deposits.
2/ Calculated both in relation to end of period and period average money holdings.
3/ Defined as the sum of end of period and beginning of period money holdings, and divided by two.

In contrast with developments in the velocity of household money, the velocity of enterprise money (Table 6), defined as gross domestic product over enterprise deposits, increased steadily after 1981. This trend could reflect a declining demand for money resulting from such factors as the increased use of inter-enterprise credits. It may also suggest an income elasticity of less than one. Alternatively, if there was excess liquidity at the beginning of the period, the observed rise in velocity may reflect a progressive reduction in excess holdings of money.

A particular problem in interpreting the behavior of monetary velocity for enterprises arises when they face a soft budget constraint, i.e., easy access to bank and inter-enterprise credit and financial relief from the government. In this context, enterprises may be less concerned with the amount of money that they happen to hold at a particular point in time than with their potential access to additional financing when they need it.

Table 6. Hungary: Velocity of Circulation of Enterprise Money

	Nominal GDP	Enterprise Deposits 1/		Velocity 2/	
		End of period	Period average 3/	End of period	Period average
	(In billions of forint)				
	(1)	(2)	(3)	(1)/(2)	(1)/(3)
1980	721.0	128.2	...	5.62	...
1981	779.9	130.1	129.2	5.99	6.04
1982	847.9	145.2	137.6	5.84	6.16
1983	896.4	130.2	137.7	6.88	6.51
1984	978.5	123.0	126.6	7.96	7.73
1985	1,033.7	138.7	130.9	7.45	7.90
1986	1,088.8	141.2	140.0	7.71	7.78
1987	1,226.4	167.0	154.1	7.34	7.96
1988	1,408.8	145.1	156.1	9.71	9.02
1989	1,730.4	211.8	178.5	8.17	9.69

Source: IMF Institute data base.

1/ All of currency in circulation is assumed to be with the household sector. Includes private enterprise deposits and deposits of financial institutions (which are small).
2/ Calculated both in relation to end of period and period average money holdings.
3/ Defined as the sum of end of period and beginning of period money holdings, and divided by two.

In assessing future movements in velocity, the stance of economic policies, whether based on unchanged policies or a more normative projection, needs to be defined as well as its implications for output, inflation, interest rates and other variables affecting the relative attractiveness of holding money as compared with other real or financial assets. Moreover, as underscored previously, it is important to identify the possible structural factors and institutional developments that could affect the demand for money, particularly as they may have the dominant influence on economic agents' behavior in a time of change.

For example, how would enterprises alter their holdings of money in response to a tighter budget constraint, including an increased threat of bankruptcy? What are the implications for the transactions demand for money of splitting large enterprises into smaller ones? How would enterprises respond to tighter credit conditions? What if forced inter-enterprise credits also were reduced?

As regards households, has the pent up demand for foreign consumer goods released by travel and partial import liberalization run its course? What impact would the September 1989 liberalization of regulations governing foreign currency deposits have on recorded levels of bank deposits (the issue being how much "under the mattress" money would flow into domestic banks)? How will households respond to the introduction of new payment and credit instruments or when faced with increased uncertainty as a result of prospective structural changes?

While quantification of these effects is no doubt difficult, it is at least important to assess the direction of change. In forecasting velocity, it should be noted that an underestimation of desired velocity, i.e., overpredicting real money demand, is likely to result in a higher inflation rate and/or a worse balance of payments outcome than programmed. On the other hand, an overestimation of desired velocity could have opposite effects. In this case the risk is that if there is some downward rigidity in prices the excess demand for money would translate into lower output growth and higher unemployment. The choice of velocity assumption in a financial program, thus, also depends on the relative importance that is attached to the inflation target as compared to the output and employment targets.

3. Forecasting the other monetary accounts

a. Net foreign assets

Projections of net foreign assets are directly linked to the prospects for the balance of payments and the availability of external financing. In a more normative scenario, the net foreign assets are targeted rather than being a passive outcome of existing policies. Abstracting from data and valuation problems, the change in net foreign assets of the banking system should be equal to the change in net international reserves (recorded, by convention, below the line in the balance of payments) and other foreign assets held by the banking system and not included in the definition of reserves (recorded above the line in the capital account of the balance of payments) minus the change in the banking system's external indebtedness (also recorded in the capital account).

In projecting the net foreign asset position for the consolidated banking system for Hungary (which is negative), it is noteworthy that in 1986–89 about 90 percent of the net foreign indebtedness of the banking system was with the NBH. This share is likely to decrease as the financial system in Hungary becomes more decentralized.

Gross foreign assets of the NBH were some 10–20 percent higher than the stock of gross international reserves in 1986-89, reflecting the exclusion of certain less liquid foreign assets from the definition of reserves. On the liability side, the NBH is the largest external debtor in Hungary. Between 1986 and 1989 its share of Hungary's total external debt remained unchanged at 86 percent.

b.   Net domestic credit

Once projections for real GDP, prices, and net foreign assets have been determined, and the estimates of the monetary aggregates have been made based on the expected behavior of the public, the amount of net domestic credit may be calculated as a residual (given some reasonable assumption with respect to the change in other items). This follows from the monetary survey identity (see Box 1). The calculated amount of net domestic credit should, nevertheless, be consistent with developments in the other sectors of the economy in the sense that the behavioral relationships among key economic variables should hold, e.g., the derived growth in credit should be consistent with projected output developments. Otherwise, a further iteration of the economic forecast across sectors will be required.

The distribution of credit among the government, state enterprises, and households is a function of policy priorities. For example, in a scenario where the policies of the government are taken as given, the amount of net credit extended to the government sector is usually dictated by the existing budgetary position of the government in relation to the cost and availability of external and nonbank financing. The credit requirements of households and enterprises could of course be accommodated more fully if the budgetary position were adjusted through revenue raising and expenditure reducing measures.

c.   Other items (net)

Other items (net), by its nature, is a difficult variable to forecast. Factors that heavily influence the movements of this variable include augmentation of the share capital of banks, e.g., to meet capital adequacy requirements, valuation changes of the net foreign asset position, and the profits/losses of the banking system.

For example, a depreciation of the forint will raise the level of net external indebtedness of the banking system, measured in local currency. Assuming no new net flows of foreign exchange, there should be no effect on the level of monetary aggregates, simply an offsetting valuation adjustment entry included in other items (the sign being positive if the foreign asset position is negative).

Losses of the banking system are recorded in other items (net) as if the banking system were extending a credit to itself, i.e., with a positive sign, the counterpart entry being a rise in monetary aggregates. In the case of profits that are not distributed but held as part of the banks' capital and reserves, it is recorded as a repayment of a credit to itself, i.e., a reduction in other items (net).

The data for Hungary show that in 1986–89, other items (net) for commercial banks remained relatively stable at minus FT 40–50 billion. This must have reflected, among other things, the transfer of most of the banks' profits to the budget. For the NBH, over the same period other items (net) was positive and increased significantly, from FT 42.6 billion in 1986 to FT 352.5 billion in 1989. The largest part of this increase was associated with valuation changes in the stock of net indebtedness.

Forecasting the Accounts of the Monetary Authorities

A typical balance sheet of the monetary authorities is shown in Box 2. The liabilities of the monetary authorities are referred to as *reserve money* (alternatively called the monetary base or high powered money). Reserve money is defined as the sum of currency outside banks plus banks' cash and deposits at the Central Bank. Variations in reserve money (R) reflect changes in the asset side of the balance sheet of the monetary authorities, which are composed of net foreign assets, (NFA), claims on the government (NDCG), claims on commercial banks (DCB), and other items net (OIN). For example, an overall surplus (deficit) in the balance of payments adds to (subtracts from) net foreign assets of the monetary authorities and, given domestic credit and other items net, increases (decreases) reserve money. Similarly, when the central bank brings about a net increase (decrease) in its assets by buying (selling) government securities or making (calling in) loans to (from) commercial banks, the increase (decrease) in these assets is typically accompanied by an increase (decrease) in reserve money.

Stylized Balance Sheet of the Monetary Authorities

Assets	Liabilities
Net foreign assets	Reserve money
	Currency outside banks
Domestic credit	Reserves of commercial
Claims on government (net)	banks
Claims on commercial	
banks	
Other items (net)	

Box 2

The central bank's control over reserve money is incomplete. For example, changes in net foreign assets, which are a reflection of the balance of payments outcome, cannot generally be considered to be a policy-controlled variable. Variations in net claims on the government are, in many countries, adjusted passively to the government's budgetary position. Typically, the most controllable factor is claims on commercial banks.

The behavior of the monetary aggregates of the consolidated banking system, as reflected in the monetary survey, can be linked to that of reserve money of the central bank by the following equation:

$$M = k\,R = k\,(NFA + NDCG + DCB + OIN) \qquad (9)$$

where:

M = monetary aggregate, however defined, of the consolidated balance sheet
k = money multiplier

If the monetary aggregate of interest in the consolidated banking system were to be broad money, then the multiplier would be derived as follows:

$$k = \frac{M}{R} = \frac{CY + DD + TD}{CY + r_d DD + r_t TD + reDD} \qquad (10)$$

where:

CY = currency outside banks
DD = demand deposits
TD = time and savings deposits
r_d = required reserve ratio against demand deposits
r_t = required reserve ratio against time and savings deposits
r_e = excess reserve as a ratio of demand deposits

Dividing the numerator and denominator by DD and defining c and b as the ratios between currency outside banks and time and savings deposits, respectively, to demand deposits:

$$= \frac{c + 1 + b}{c + r_d + br_t + re} \qquad (11)$$

Equation (11) indicates that the value of the money multiplier reflects the behavior of three different types of economic agents: (1) the monetary authorities who set the reserve requirements; (2) the general public who, given the structure of interest rates and other variables, determines the composition of the money stock, e.g., the amount of currency held relative to deposits; and (3) the commercial banks who decide on how much excess reserves to hold. Table 7 suggests that after the formal establishment of a two-tier banking system, the multiplier for broad money in Hungary was relatively stable at about 1.9.

To summarize, the money supply process, as captured by equation (9), is influenced both by central bank actions, such as changes in claims on commercial banks and reserve requirements. However, it also reflects developments in the balance of payments (NFA), the behavior of government (NDCG), commercial banks (re) and nonbank public (c). These developments need to be explicitly considered when forecasting and seeking to control the money supply.

	Broad money	Reserve money	Money multiplier
Table 7. Hungary: Reserve Money and Money Multipliers			
	(In billions of forint)		
	(1)	(2)	(3) = (1)/(2)
1983	410.5	324.2	1.27
1984	432.3	289.2	1.49
1985	480.8	330.1	1.46
1986	524.7	352.2	1.49
1987	582.0	313.4	1.86
1988	593.7	299.3	1.98
1989	665.6	358.1	1.86

Source: IMF Institute data base.

Exercises and Issues for Discussion

1. Exercises

a.   Complete the monetary survey and the accounts of the NBH for 1990 as shown in Tables 8 and 9. Specifically,

- Projections of the net foreign asset position and net credit extended to the general government should be consistent with forecasts made in the other workshops on the balance of payments and the fiscal accounts.

- Factors affecting the demand for money (including interest rate policy) and the share of currency in broad money should be explicitly assessed.

- Consideration should be given to the expected value of the money multiplier and the implied changes in the central bank's balance sheet relative to past trends.

- Given the size of other items (net), estimates of valuation changes of the net foreign liability position should be undertaken. For simplicity, it can be assumed that the currency composition of the net foreign liability position is the same as the SDR basket.

- While credit to the nongovernment sector may be calculated as a residual, it should, nevertheless, be consistent with expected developments in prices and output. Some iteration with other workshops may be needed to achieve this.

2. Issues for discussion

a.   Review the main factors that were taken into account in estimating the demand for money. What importance was attached to structural factors?

b.   Discuss the instruments of monetary control underlying your scenario. What would be the implications of the money multiplier being larger than projected? How could this come about?

c.   Relative to your scenario, what are the implications for monetary policy of an improvement in the balance of payments? What might be an appropriate policy response to this situation?

d.   Discuss the main weaknesses of the financial system at end 1989. What measures could be taken to strengthen it?

200

e.   What would be the implications of a liquidity overhang for the conduct of monetary policy?

f.   What are the implications of currency substitution, i.e., switching money holdings out of local currency into foreign currency, for the conduct of economic policies? Is this a problem that you would foresee for Hungary?

Table 8. Hungary: Monetary Survey

(In billions of forint, end of period)

	1982	1983	1984	1985	1986	1987	1988	1989	1990 Reference
Net foreign assets	-336.9	-386.4	-427.8	-451.9	-574.5	-728.3	-830.2	-1074.1	
Net domestic credit	742.8	808.5	887.1	963.4	1134.1	1363.7	1483.7	1806.5	
General government (net)	298.1	302.3	291.5	294.4	352.8	403.1	410.6	465.6	
State enterprises	276.8	284.2	300.3	327.5	367.1	389.9	382.8	464.4	
Private entrepreneurs	2.5	3.1	4.0	4.6	5.1	6.9	8.6	18.5	
Financial institutions 1/	133.4	135.7	148.2	149.6	147.5	180.2	208.9	238.2	
Households	131.0	151.1	175.5	200.5	230.0	265.2	296.9	313.5	
Other items (net)	-99.0	-67.9	-32.4	-13.2	31.6	118.4	175.9	306.3	
Of which:									
valuation changes	...	31.4	40.9	43.2	106.2	196.3	249.5	460.7	
Liabilities to nongovernment	405.9	422.1	459.3	511.5	559.6	635.4	653.5	732.4	
Broad money	397.7	410.5	432.3	480.8	524.7	582.0	593.7	665.6	
Currency in circulation	84.9	94.8	105.4	116.7	130.7	153.7	164.4	180.5	
Household deposits	167.6	185.5	203.9	225.4	252.8	261.3	284.2	273.3	
State enterprise deposits	142.6	126.6	117.7	137.1	135.0	158.9	138.7	174.8	
Private enterprise deposits	—	—	—	—	—	—	...	23.9	
Financial institutions' deposits 1/	2.6	3.6	5.3	1.6	6.2	8.1	6.4	13.1	
Bonds and savings notes	8.2	11.6	27.0	30.7	34.9	53.4	59.8	66.8	

(In percentage change, unless otherwise indicated)

Memorandum items:									
Credit									
Including other items		8.8	9.7	8.6	17.7	20.2	8.8	21.8	
Excluding other items		4.1	4.9	6.2	12.9	13.0	5.0	14.7	
Of which:									
State enterprises	...	2.7	5.7	9.1	12.1	6.2	-1.8	21.3	
Household sector	...	15.3	16.1	14.2	14.7	15.3	12.0	5.6	
General government (change in relation to GDP)	...	0.5	0.1	0.3	5.4	4.1	0.5	3.2	
Broad money	...	3.2	5.3	11.2	9.1	10.9	2.0	12.1	
GDP growth	...	5.7	9.2	5.6	5.3	12.6	14.9	22.8	

Source: IMF Institute data base.

1/ Mainly State Development Bank.

Table 9. Hungary: Accounts of the National Bank of Hungary

(In billions of forint, end of period)

	1983	1984	1985	1986	1987	1988	1989	1990 Reference	1990 Program
Net foreign assets	-340.5	-382.2	-411.6	-524.4	-677.0	-774.4	-954.3		
Foreign assets	91.0	121.3	172.7	159.8	138.3	138.6	162.7		
Less: Foreign liabilities	431.5	503.5	584.3	684.2	815.3	913.0	1117.0		
Domestic credit	664.7	671.4	741.7	876.6	990.4	1073.7	1312.4		
Central government (including State Development Bank) 1/	440.6	440.1	446.0	502.7	577.5	619.7	706.7		
Commercial banks 2/	--	--	--	--	253.8	225.4	252.1		
Other residents (net)	238.8	255.4	294.7	331.3	2.0	4.6	1.1		
Other items (net)	-14.7	-24.1	1.0	42.6	157.1	224.0	352.5		
Reserve money	324.2	289.2	330.1	352.2	313.4	299.3	358.1		

Source: IMF Institute data base.

1/ Note that this line closely approximates the sum of credits extended to the general government and to financial institutions in the monetary survey.
2/ Refinancing credits.

Table 10. Hungary: International Reserves and Other Foreign Assets

(In millions of U.S. dollars, end of period)

	1982	1983	1984	1985	1986	1987	1988	1989
International reserves in convertible currencies	941.9	1576.9	2026.1	2792.5	3053.0	2159.2	1976.3	1725.3
Gold 1/	213.4	367.9	504.7	639.9	750.6	525.1	509.7	479.1
Foreign exchange	728.5	1209.0	1521.4	2152.6	2302.4	1634.1	1466.6	1246.2
Nonconvertible currencies 2/	58.0	45.0	43.0	224.6	174.2	289.4	201.9	567.1
Total international reserves	999.9	1621.9	2069.1	3017.1	3227.2	2448.6	2178.2	2292.4
Other foreign assets								
Convertible currencies 3/	2007.3	2174.5	2408.2	3116.4	3185.9	3741.7	3659.9	3764.6
Nonconvertible currencies	395.2	430.0	384.0	422.1	481.0	523.5	501.7	669.0
Total international reserves and other foreign assets	3402.4	4226.4	4861.3	6555.6	6894.1	6713.8	6339.8	6726.0
Memorandum items:								
Change in convertible currency international reserves		635.0	449.2	766.4	260.5	-893.8	-182.9	-251.0
Change in nonconvertible international reserves		-13.0	-2.0	181.6	-50.4	115.2	-87.5	365.2

Source: IMF Institute data base.

1/ Actual holdings of gold, at national valuation of US$4275 per fine troy ounce from 1982 to 1985, and US$4320 per troy ounce from 1986.

2/ Valued at the official exchange rates.

3/ Mainly trade credit extended by Hungarian enterprises.

Table 11. Hungary: Outstanding External Debt

(In millions of U.S. dollars, at end of period)

	1982	1983	1984	1985	1986	1987	1988	1989
Total external debt	11,515	12,125	12,216	15,106	17,928	20,531	20,150	20,966
In convertible currencies	10,216	10,746	10,983	13,955	16,907	19,584	19,603	20,605
By original maturity								
Short-term	3,261	3,904	2,977	3,019	3,494	3,103	3,363	3,306
Medium- and long-term	6,955	6,842	8,006	10,936	13,413	16,481	16,240	17,299
By type of credit:								
Financial loans	9,155	9,208	9,428	12,175	15,084	17,508	17,469	18,060
Trade-related credits	661	1,144	1,125	1,318	1,433	1,652	1,626	1,763
Intergovernment credits	5	4	3	2	1	0	--	--
Other	396	390	428	459	389	422	508	568
In nonconvertible currencies	1,299	1,379	1,233	1,151	1,021	947	547	361
By original maturity								
Short-term	250	367	916	106	111	184	120	87
Medium- and long-term	1,049	1,012	317	1,045	910	763	427	274
By type of credit:								
Financial loans	251	366	313	133	140	210	136	88
Trade-related credits	39	30	24	0	--	--	--	--
Intergovernment credits	974	948	863	1,009	873	728	438	260
Other	35	38	32	8	8	8	8	12
Memorandum item:								
Convertible currency debt 1/								
(as percent of GDP)	44.1	51.1	53.9	67.7	71.2	75.0	70.1	70.3

Source: IMF Institute data base

1/ End of period convertible currency external debt divided by GDP for the year as a whole in local currency units and converted into U.S. Dollars at the period average forint/U.S. Dollar exchange rate.